2019 Edition

Second Printing, August 2019

Metrics Reporting, Inc.
7063 Country Springs Drive
Byron Center, MI 4931

Metrics Reporting, Inc. (MRI) designs processes and tools for workforce professionals. Our focus is to provide pragmatic tools and guidance for working professionals to help them implement demand-driven, evidence-based talent systems that align with nationally recognized policy and best practices. We share our work via research briefs, guidebooks, and various project specific websites. Please visit www.metricsreporting.com to learn more about our work and to find links to projects and publications.

We extend our impact by licensing our intellectual property (IP) to other organizations and individuals. Examples include the **Skilling America** training and credentialing initiative by Hope Street Group, the **SkillsFirst** career pathway software platform by Think Optimal, and our **Talxcellenz**® website that supports job analysts to conduct O*NET-Based Confirmatory Job Analysis Process.

The overarching goal in our work is to help individuals prepare, secure, and retain good jobs. We want to help people build and clearly articulate their skills, so they stand out from the crowd. Our cover images illustrate that concept.

The information contained within this handbook should not be construed as legal advice, in any manner and specifically within employment and labor law. The authors of this document are not lawyers. This handbook is meant to assist individuals who interact with job seekers on a regular basis. Practitioners should seek the advice of legal counsel whenever appropriate in order to ensure that activities undertaken as part of this guidebook are consistent with local, state, and federal law.

66 The Career Navigation System (CNS) is the heart of the MRI career pathways model. This is the place where educators and workforce professionals will find the straightforward tools they need to deliver high quality services to individual participants. The CNS connects evidence-based competencies and individual career paths so that people can enter into and advance through good jobs. 99

- James Guest, Director of Research
Metrics Reporting, Inc.

METRICS REPORTING
Talent SCM Systems

3	4	
1	2	

MRI Career Pathways Model

System	Regional Industry Sector Strategies	Career Navigation System (CNS)	Job Analysis and Validation (JAV)
Books	Stakeholder Guidebook	**Career Navigation System Guidebook**	Job Analysis Guidebook
Content Areas	• Customers & Stakeholders • Collective Impact • Regional Work Plan • Organization & Communication • Supply-Demand • Competency Signals • Career Pathways • Career Coaching • Career Profiles • Funding	• Introduction, Theory, & Practice • Process, Tools, & Outcomes • Career Coaching • Education, Training, Credentialing, and Licensing • Career Profiles	• Job Grouping • Job Analysis • Occupational Competencies • Credentials • Foundational Competencies • Validation

Table of Contents

Dedication 9

MRI Forward 11

Section I **Introduction, Theory, and Purpose** 12
Chapter 1: Introduction 15
Chapter 2: Theory of Change 21
Chapter 3: Overview of the Career Navigation System Guidebook 27

Section II **Evidence-Based Career Coaching** 32
Chapter 4: Career Coaching Process 35
Chapter 5: Career Coaching Tools 47
Chapter 6: Career Coaching Technology (Assessments) 121

Section III **Education, Training, & Credentials** 132
Chapter 7: Foundational Skills, Measures, and Credentials 135
Chapter 8: Employability Skills and Credentials 143
Chapter 9: Occupational Skills and Credentials 145
Chapter 10: Industry-Wide Skills and Credentials 151
Chapter 11: Credentials, Degrees, and Licenses 153

Section IV **Evidence-Based Career Profiles** 156
Chapter 12: Assembling the Career Profile 159
Chapter 13: The Use of Assessments in Career Profiles 163
Chapter 14: Career Profile Outputs 171

Appendices **Resources & Tools** 178
A: Glossary 181
B: Sources and Recommendations 193
C: Joint Letter on Career Pathways (2016) 199
D: ETS WorkFORCE Assessment for Cognitive Ability 203
E: ETS WorkFORCE Assessment for Job Fit 207
F: ETS WorkFORCE Assessment for Career Development 211

Dedication - Mr. Tom Karel, 1949-2015

Tom Karel was the vice president and chief human resources officer at Mercy Health Saint Mary's, a Regional Health Ministry of Trinity Health. Tom was the executive sponsor of our work and supported it immensely.

I had the privilege of working very closely with Tom over the last ten years. Initially we worked together on community workforce projects and most recently on projects for Mercy Health. We literally had a shared vision. In October 2010, we first published it in a paper titled Talent SCM 2025 Vision. The paper documented our vision of an ideal talent system in the year 2025 where workforce agencies, educational institutions, and employers work together seamlessly so every individual has a path to a great job.

Allow me to share with you five lessons from Tom:

- He taught us about **courage** – Tom was courageous. He had the courage to imagine a better world, an ideal world, and he worked tirelessly to bring it about.
- He taught us about **teamwork** – Tom believed in his team. He believed that they could be the very best; that they could find national best practices, implement them, improve them, and become the example for others to follow. He set the bar high and none of us ever questioned it.
- He taught us about **noble purpose** – Tom believed everyone could and should find their noble purpose – that place where people experience extraordinary joy in serving others.
- He taught us about **meaningful work** – Tom saw work as a source of great joy and life satisfaction. Everyone needs to find a joyful and satisfying place to work; a place where we can live lives of noble purpose.
- He taught us that **everyone belongs** – Tom believed everyone belongs somewhere. Leadership isn't about sorting out the good ones from the bad ones and sending the bad ones away. Great leadership starts with the understanding that every life matters. We need to help people discover where they belong and help them along the path to get there.

We carry on this great work recognizing Tom's contributions.

- Bill Guest, August 2016

Forward

In our time as students of workforce strategy, we have seen that the last decade was one of marvelous innovation in the U.S. workforce system. Great progress was made advancing sector strategies, career coaching, and career pathways models. Thankfully, much that was learned in this decade has influenced the Workforce Innovation and Opportunity Act (WIOA) and we can enter into the next round of innovation. We see this as a great opportunity to work together to continue to improve our workforce development system so that it delivers qualified candidates to employers and provides a clear path to meaningful, well paying jobs.

James Guest
Metrics Reporting, Inc.
Director of Research
james.guest@metricsreporting.com

We have learned much and had great success working with employers building evidence-based models. Our evidence-based selection process has delivered a diverse high quality workforce: first-year turnover is down, diversity is up. Most recently we expanded the evidence-based system to include career pathways and career profiles in partnership with WIOA agencies, community colleges, and other community partners. This guidebook introduces the processes and tools that enable practitioners to build evidence-based career navigation systems.

Steven Bennett
Humanity 2.0
Founder & Chair
steve@humanity2point0.org

We thank everyone that contributed to the many papers we have read over the last decade. Your efforts to organize and publish your successes have enabled this work. Many sources are listed in Appendix B, and some of the most relevant are specifically mentioned at the end of various chapters in a section titled "Dig Deeper."

Bill Guest
Metrics Reporting, Inc.
President & Chief Solutions Architect
bill.guest@metricsreporting.com

Lastly, we welcome your feedback. Please don't hesitate to contact us.

Section I

Introduction, Theory, & Purpose

"...This approach will result in a fully aligned, demand-driven talent supply chain that increases economic opportunity for individuals and supports employer talent objectives."

empowering the
whole individual

ASPIRATIONS

Incorporating aspirations is paramount in ensuring long-term success for the individual.

CAREER PATH

A defined career path provides the tools necessary for an individual to succeed.

SKILLS

Defining the skills an individual needs for a defined career path is essential.

COMPETENCIES

Ensuring an individual achieves competencies that are aligned with their career path helps create success for the individual and the employer.

CREDENTIALS

Obtaining stackable credentials throughout one's defined career path helps ensure long-term success and upward mobility in the workforce.

SECURITY

Aligning efforts to empower the whole individual creates opportunities for individual economic security.

Chapter 1

Introduction

Sector initiatives and career pathways work for people. Over the last decade many fine organizations have developed, demonstrated, and documented that sector strategies and career pathways are effective ways to serve the sourcing and hiring needs of employers and to increase economic opportunity for individuals. Those same organizations have published various frameworks and advocacy documents that have been extremely helpful to many of us. What we find lacking are good "how to" guides to help regions do the work once they have accepted sector initiatives and career pathways as viable strategies. This book is one of a series of guidebooks by the Metrics Reporting, Inc. (MRI), each of which is designed to help practitioners implement these strategies in their own regions. These books include:

- The Stakeholder Guidebook
- The Job Analysis Guidebook
- The Subject Matter Expert Workbook (forthcoming)
- The Career Navigation System Guidebook
- The Career Pathway Participant Workbook (forthcoming)
- The Educator Guide (forthcoming)

Check for updated versions and new books at our website – www.metricsreporting.com – and amazon.com.

This Career Navigation System Guidebook is primarily for the practitioners in workforce agencies and community colleges that help individuals find their path to economic security and family-sustaining jobs. In the introductory chapters in Section 1, however, we offer an overview of the essential elements in an evidence-based career pathways system.

Key Roles

The key roles in this work include the sector facilitator, career coaches, caseworkers, and job analysts.

Sector Facilitators

While it may go by many other names, this role leads the collective efforts of the industry sector and is likely, but not necessarily, housed in the backbone organization of a sector initiative. The sector facilitator is the primary employer-facing role. As such, he or she facilitates the agreements between the backbone organization, employers, education and training providers, and community partners.

Job Analysts

Job analysts will plan and conduct regional consortia-style job analysis and validation studies. Without good information, demand-driven solutions are based on beliefs, wishes or hunches rather than knowledge supported by evidence. The role of the job analyst is to collect and examine the information necessary to define and validate the competencies that can be measurably related to job performance.

Caseworkers

Caseworkers support each participant's journey from beginning to end. They guide selected participants into the career coaching process at the appropriate time and support participants' referrals to employers with completed career profiles. To succeed in matching those individuals with jobs in which they will excel and flourish, caseworkers need the information supplied by job analysis and competency validation.

Career Coaches

Career coaches facilitate the career coaching process at the front end of the career pathway. Coaches use assessments to help individuals gain an accurate view of self and they support the participant's progress through career exploration, decision making, and action planning steps. Career coaches will likely be housed at multiple institutions and community partners throughout the region. Like caseworkers, career coaches need an evidence-based career pathway model to succeed in getting individuals the education and training

they need to attain the competencies required by employers, and to guide individuals into and along career pathways.

Overview of Stakeholders in Career Pathway Systems

While the activities described in this guidebook are primarily focused on the work of workforce practitioners, it is useful to have a sense of the stakeholders potentially involved in a fully developed career pathway system.

The stakeholders involved in a career pathway or sector initiative generally include the following four major groups (On this list, each major group is broken down into sub-groups and just a few of many possible examples are mentioned. The roles discussed are typical arrangements, but there is no set formula for stakeholder engagement, and roles will vary by region):

Employers: Employers will likely play a leading role in providing talent supply/demand data and defining occupational and foundational skill requirements and measures. They may also be highly engaged in building the regional talent supply chain, career coaching and navigation, education and training support, support services, job search and placement, and the development of apprenticeship, internship or externship programs.

- Employers: small, medium, large employers.
- Employer Associations: Chambers of Commerce, Industry Associations, Membership Organizations, etc.

Individuals: MRI aims to move individuals into and along career pathways by aligning employer and education signals. Individuals need to be able to track employer competency signals, navigate the talent supply chain to develop those competencies, and benefit from regional communication and engagement.

- Youth: K–12 students, Disengaged Youth.
- Adults: Disconnected, Unemployed, Underemployed.
- Employees: Low-wage workers, Incumbents.

Providers: Education and training providers, including workforce agencies, will likely be responsible for driving collective impact, obtaining funding, and

leading regional communication and engagement; and they will be highly engaged in obtaining talent supply/demand data and defining occupational and foundational competency requirements with employers. Various other providers may play leading roles or be highly engaged in building the regional talent supply chain, career coaching and navigation, education and training support, support services, job search and placement, and the development of apprenticeship, internship or externship programs.

- Workforce Agencies (Public Agencies, Workforce Intermediaries, American Job Centers).
- Education (Community Colleges, Public Universities, For-Profit Schools, Career and Technical Education).
- Others (Workforce Training, Adult Education, Academic and Career Navigation, Literacy Centers, GED/High School Equivalency Organizations)

Publics: While public bodies will likely not play a leading role, various publics may play a highly engaged role in driving collective impact, offering support services, and providing funding opportunities. Publics may also play a supporting role in providing talent supply/demand data and defining occupational and foundational skill requirements and measures. Policy and advocacy groups in particular play a supporting role in building the talent supply chain.

- State Government (Workforce Agency, Health and Human Services, Governor's Office, Workforce Board)
- Local Government (City, County, Workforce Agency, Health and Human Services)
- Policy and Advocacy (Workforce Advocates, Poverty Advocates, Low-wage Worker Advocates).
- NGOs (Economic Development Organizations, Community Organizations, Faith-Based Organizations, Philanthropy)

The backbone agency will be responsible for convening the other participants and ensuring that all community partners have the tools and resources needed to help their region build career pathways. It will also serve as the collective voice of the initiative and may also serve as the quality assurance agent, helping

to ensure that both employers and job seekers are served in the best way possible.

Dig Deeper

See Appendix A for an extensive glossary. Much of the research on career pathways emphasizes the need for a common vocabulary. To advance this goal, our glossary includes a number of terms pulled from similarly extensive glossaries in two of the most widely recognized guidebooks:

- DOL (2016), Career Pathways Toolkit.
- AQCP CLASP (2014), Shared Visions, Strong Systems, Appendix C, pp. 37–42.

On stakeholders in various career pathway models, see also:

- Corporation for a Skilled Workforce CSW (2014), Call for a National Conversation on Creating a Competency-based Credentialing Ecosystem. See pp. 6-7 for stakeholder roles, and Appendix A (pp. 8-10) for current roles in the system.
- DOL (2016), Career Pathways Toolkit. See Element 1 on building cross-agency pathways.
- US Chamber of Commerce Foundation (USCCF) (2015), Building the Talent Pipeline: An Implementation Guide. See pp. 36–39 on aligning incentives among stakeholders.
- USCCF (2014), Managing the Talent Pipeline: An Implementation Guide. See pp. 14-19 on implications for employers, 20-23 for education and workforce, 24-27 for students and workers, and 28-30 for policymakers.
- (CSW) (2013), Making a Market for Competency Based Credentials, p. 4, pp. 25–29.
- Jobs for the Future (JFF) (2012), The Promise of Career Pathway Systems Change, pp. 15–23. See especially the chart on p. 20.

Chapter 2

Theory of Change

Recent debate about the "skills gap" suggests that traditional labor pools for talent are not enough to fill all open positions. Whatever the extent and causes of the skills gap may be, we believe that a competency-based signaling problem between employers on the one hand and individuals and providers on the other is a contributing factor to it. Some employers are sending inaccurate, weak or confusing signals to their talent supply chains. MRI provides an evidence-based approach and methodology to clearly define the competencies required to be successful in jobs so that employers, individuals, providers and publics are all aware of the competencies needed to obtain a job, perform successfully, and advance.

MRI aims to assist in the development of pipelines so that qualified individuals fill vacancies and are able to advance in their careers. This goal can be achieved by leveraging standard practices in industrial/organizational psychology and open databases such the O*NET in order to define, link and validate the occupational and foundational competencies that are measurably related to job performance. This information can then guide sourcing, hiring and development strategies by employers, the improvement of career coaching strategies, and the development of curriculum by education and training providers.

We call this approach Talent Excellence; this approach will result in a fully aligned, demand-driven talent supply chain that increases economic opportunity for individuals and supports employer talent objectives. Based on our prior experience, the Talent Excellence approach results in fewer vacancies, lower turnover rates (a proxy for higher employee quality), and higher diversity rates for employers.

Collective Impact

Collective Impact is a framework for social change that we have used to develop regional career pathways. It is characterized by the commitment of a group of actors from different sectors to a common agenda for solving a specific social problem, using a structured form of collaboration. The approach of collective impact is placed in contrast to "isolated impact," in which organizations primarily work alone to solve social problems. MRI believes that collective impact is the optimal strategy to develop and implement effective career pathways and talent pipelines.

Initiatives must meet five criteria in order to be considered collective impact (Kania and Kramer, "Collective Impact," Stanford Social Innovation Review, Winter 2011):

- **Common Agenda:** All participating organizations (government agencies, non-profits, community members, etc.) have a shared vision for social change that includes a common understanding of the problem and a joint approach to solving the problem through agreed upon actions.
- **Shared Measurement System:** Agreement on the ways success will be measured and reported with a short list of key indicators across all participating organizations.
- **Mutually Reinforcing Activities:** Engagement of a diverse set of stakeholders, typically across sectors, coordinating a set of differentiated activities through a mutually reinforcing plan of action.
- **Continuous Communication:** Frequent communications over a long period of time among key players within and across organizations, to build trust and inform ongoing learning and adaptation of strategy.
- **Backbone Organization:** Ongoing support provided by an independent staff dedicated to the initiative. The backbone staff tends to play six roles to move the initiative forward: Guide Vision and Strategy; Support Aligned Activity; Establish Shared Measurement Practices; Build Public Will; Advance Policy; and Mobilize Funding.

MRI Competency Framework

Competencies provide a framework to define job requirements and evaluate job readiness of candidates. They help reduce and eliminate barriers to employment

for individuals, including individuals from underrepresented groups and those deemed hard to serve, and they help employers better articulate how individuals can attain long-term economic security.

While we recognize that many organizations have published various useful competency models, the following model is helpful for organizing discussions and agreements around competencies:

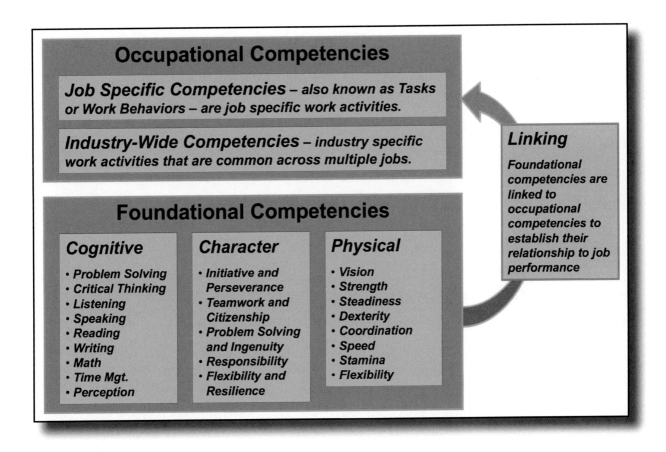

This model has two main parts: occupational competencies and foundational competencies.

- Occupational competencies are mainly represented by nationally portable occupational credentials that are developed and maintained by credentialing organizations in the sector. Credentialing organizations may be professional associations, industry organizations, or others. Occupational competencies can be sub-divided into job-specific and industry-wide competencies.

- Foundational competencies refer to cognitive, character and physical abilities and are sometimes referred to as "soft skills." To qualify as "evidence-based," they should be determined by job analysis and confirmed by validation studies, not simply by discussion and consensus.

Credentials are generally associated with occupational competencies. The best credentialing organizations engage industrial psychologists to perform a job analysis that provides detailed occupational competency information. This information then becomes a basis for curriculum, accreditation, assessment, credentialing, and continuing education.

Very few foundational skills credentials have achieved wide use within or across sectors. Yet foundational competencies are often very good predictors of job performance. It is therefore important to identify which foundational competencies can be measurably linked to the occupational competencies. Establishing this link requires job analysis.

There is an inherent expectation that credentials and employment tests are predictive of job performance. Validation studies therefore include analysis of quantitative data. Specifically, validation quantifies the relationship between what a test actually measures and what it is intended to measure or predict.

The term "validation" is used in two ways. Employers validate the use of assessments by conducting validation studies that confirm competencies are job-related – that is, related to job performance ratings. Validation studies ensure that measures of those competencies will be predictive of job performance. Testing firms validate that assessments measure the competencies that they are targeted to measure, and this ensures that the assessments are useful to employers and individuals as proof of job-related skills. The best systems will require both validation of job-related competencies by employers and assessment tools by test firms.

Career Pathways

Competencies, career pathways and stackable credentials are separate but related concepts. Sometimes the term "stackable credentials" is used interchangeably with "career pathways," but they are not the same. The

USDOL and the Alliance for Quality Career Pathways (AQCP, part of CLASP) define a stackable credential as "part of a sequence of credentials that can be accumulated over time to build individuals' qualifications and help them move on along a career pathway up a career ladder to different and potentially higher paying jobs." Therefore, stackable credentials correspond only to what AQCP calls the first feature of a career pathway (well connected and transparent education, training, credentialing, and support service offerings). The connection between career pathways and competencies is competency-based stackable credentials and competency-based employment assessments.

The Career Navigation System included in the MRI career pathways model supports individuals through career coaching, education and training experiences, and a career profile to help individuals earn credentials as they advance along a career path. The underlying idea is that a good career is a series of good jobs. Individuals run this sequence for each job transition.

Employment Market Innovation

Markets are generally most efficient when they are transparent, when both buyer and seller are aware of the transaction details. In the case of the employment marketplace, the market works best when employers are transparent and communicate job requirements clearly and accurately. This means employers need to identify, analyze and validate the competencies that are related to job performance. They should require the credentials and assessment scores for those competencies. Individuals too need to be transparent. Individuals should present credentials and assessment scores that are accurate reflections of their qualifications for the job.

Social innovation at the macro level is largely accomplished within states and regions. National efforts frequently engage the programs already underway in states and regions. In this way, the 50 states are collectively a kind of innovation lab for the federal government. Federal departments and agencies can provide resources to target particular national needs and observe state outcomes to determine which states are most effective. The most effective states can then be held up as models. Our project is designed to innovate at the regional (or site) level rather than at the state level. This regional level innovation is symbiotic with the state level innovation that exists in the U.S.

The use of foundational competencies, occupational credentials, and career pathways as part of a comprehensive workforce strategy provides the opportunity to test, implement, and improve innovative sourcing and hiring mechanisms that can alleviate the shortage of qualified talent in sectors across the nation. To that end, MRI is built on the premise that the convergence of community partners, employers, and job seekers should result in the use of best practices that lead to long-term economic security for the individual, the sector, and the employer community.

Dig Deeper

- On the collective impact model, see the original and authoritative article: Kania, J. and Kramer, M. (Winter 2011) "Collective Impact," Stanford Social Innovation Review, pp. 36–41.
- For comprehensive guides to career pathways, see Shared Vision, Strong Systems, Framework Version 1.0, June 2014 published by Alliance for Quality Career Pathways, a project of CLASP; and
- Career Pathways Toolkit, Six Key Elements for Success, September 2011 (updated 2015 in light of WIOA legislation), developed on behalf of the U.S. Department of Labor by Social Policy Research Associates

Chapter 3

Overview of the Career Navigation System Guidebook

This handbook is designed to provide employers, workforce agencies, and community partners with the tools necessary to support job seekers wishing to build a career pathway. The tools and processes recommended here are aligned with the demand-driven, evidence-based approach to career pathways described in the MRI Stakeholder Guidebook, and the processes and tools described in the Job Analysis Guidebook that are used to document foundational and occupational competencies measurably related to job performance. This book is primarily for the career coaches and caseworkers that wish to make use of that data to help individuals find their own path to family-sustaining wage jobs.

This guidebook supports a set of strategies that will consistently produce a diverse and qualified workforce. This specific guidebook supports the development of effective career navigation systems that help individuals enter into and advance through entry-level jobs to obtain middle skills jobs. This guidebook includes:

- A comprehensive and straightforward career coaching process.
- A clear view of participants' intended experience .
- A clear view of the value to stakeholders gained by using assessments and other evidence-based methods to guide career coaching activities organized in 6 process steps and 34 supporting tools.
- A clear view of the value to stakeholders gained by using assessments and other evidence-based methods to document the skills of job seekers.

Workforce organizations and community colleges may serve as the organizing

agency by which collective efforts in support of this work can converge. As the "backbone" supporting agency, these organizations ensure that all community partners have the tools and resources needed to help their stakeholders build family-sustaining careers. The backbone organization can also serve as the quality control agent, helping to ensure that job seekers are served in the best way possible. No matter what kind of organization serves as the backbone agency, this lead organization should be positioned to leverage the contributions of community partners who already do much of the work described in this handbook. By leveraging existing work, much of which is best practice, communities and regions around the country can build strong local talent pipelines for employers in each sector.

This guidebook, like every MRI guidebook, is intended to provide ideas and strategies to leverage or improve existing practice. The goal is to build upon your regional successes, not to replace current practices with new ones. The tools and processes recommended within can be used to compliment and enhance the coaching efforts of workforce agencies and community colleges in your region. The Career Profile framework can be used to enhance the job referral processes currently in practice in your region. We have studied and want to build on the excellent work that has been done developing sector strategies and career pathways across America over the last decade.

Career Navigation Process Overview

Apart from these introductory chapters (Part I), the book has three parts that correspond to the core pieces of the career navigation system. In Part II we discuss evidence-based Career Coaching; in Part III we look at Education, Training and Credentialing; and in Part IV we discuss the evidence-based Career Profile.

These latter three parts correspond, at the highest level, to the typical journey an individual will take when making a career transition. This journey is illustrated on the chart on the next page.

(Start)	Career Navigation System	(Finish)
Career Coaching	Education, Training, & Credentials	Career Profile
Find the best next step	Learn and earn credentials	Connect with employers
• Preparation • Self-Awareness • Option Exploration • Decision Making • Action Planning • Follow-Up	• Career Foundations • Industry-Wide Competencies • Occupational Competencies • Degrees, Credentials, & Licensing	• Proactive Planning • Preparation for Strong Interview Performance • Prove It: Attestation of Job-Related Skills

Of course, the traditional manner of seeking, applying, and interviewing for an open position is always available to individuals. However, those that seek additional assistance in their quest for a career or wish to be guaranteed an interview (our recommendation) with a participating regional employer can follow the career navigation process described in this guidebook. Visually, we view this process in a systemic manner:

Work

Work is an essential part of well-being. Work-based learning is an essential form of development.

Job Transition

The job transition will likely occur multiple times for all individuals as they earn stackable credentials and advance their careers.

Coaching

Evidence-based **career coaching** includes assessments to better align skills, abilities, and aspirations for the individual.

Profile

The development of a **career profile** helps prepare individuals for careers now and in the future.

Training

Individuals need to complete some post-secondary **education**, **training**, and **credentials** in order to compete for good jobs.

career navigation system

In outline, the process consists of the following participant steps:

- *Compelling or catalyzing event.* An individual seeking employment or a next step in their career initiates the career navigation process through engagement with a community partner or workforce agency.
- *Initiate career coaching.* Coaching helps individuals find their best next step that results in job targets and an education or training strategy to attain them.
- *Career Coaching.* Complete the four main components of the career coaching process: self-awareness, option exploration, decision-making, and action planning.
- *Education & Training.* Individuals then pursue the education or training needed to earn the required credentials for their target occupation.
- *Quality control.* Career coaches stay in touch with individuals as they complete their training, build a career profile, and confirm job readiness before connecting the individual with an employer.
- *Career Profile.* Individuals connect with employers and demonstrate their achievements in an evidence-based career profile.
- *Interview with Employer.* Once the career profile is complete, the local backbone agency (community partner or workforce agency) forwards the individual on for an interview with the employer, bypassing traditional filters and positioning the individual for maximum consideration.
- *Accept Position, Restart Process, or Initiate Intervention Steps.* If the individual is offered employment, the regular hiring and on-boarding process for employment begins. If not, the individual and the community partner will review other possible open positions or develop intervention strategies.
- *Follow-up.* The community partner and workforce agency will conduct general follow-up activities with each individual, as appropriate, based on the local operating agreement for each region. Having developed an understanding of one's own career pathway, individuals can repeat this process as they move from job one to job two and beyond.

The 7-Step Career Pathways Model

The following model provides a framework for regional collaboration.

Intake > Coaching > Support > Learning > Credentials > Profiles > Placement

A / **B**

1. **Intake** – A coordinated regional intake process
2. **Coaching** – Evidence-based career coaching
3. **Support** – Braided funding for financial support and coordinated wrap-around services
4. **Learning** – Education, training, and work-based learning
5. **Credentials** – Certificates, degrees, certifications, and licenses
6. **Profiles** – Evidence-based career profiles
7. **Placement** – Employer defined requirements and referral of qualified candidates

In the spirit of innovation, this career navigation system will contribute to the development of a region's broader talent supply chain for their local employers in ways that are currently relatively uncommon. In particular, this book is about how to use assessments and other evidence-based methods to support career navigation. Assessments help employers make better hiring decisions; and they help individuals understand their personal value in the jobs marketplace. The paradigm shift created by the use of evidence-based career profiles is that an employer recognizes a career profile holder is serious about their work and career choice, and employers should be led to ask, "Where might this applicant fit with us?" As described in the MRI Stakeholder Guidebook, the collaborative efforts of all stakeholders will help develop an even more qualified and diverse workforce for any sector or region.

Section II

Evidence-Based Career Coaching

"The goal of the career coaching process is to guide participants from awareness of the program, to knowledge of education requirements and job options, and finally to full control over their career path."

START

evidence-based
career coaching

PREPARATION

P

Participants become aware of the overall career coaching process.

Participants complete assessments, resumes, career histories, and investigate interests.

01 **SELF-UNDERSTANDING**

CAREER EXPLORATION

02

Participants develop defined career interests and explore O*NET online.

Participants, using evidence, make informed decisions to create a career path.

 03 **DECISION MAKING**

ACTION PLANS

04

Participants develop an action plan focused on education, training, and work readiness.

FINISH **FOLLOW-UP**

Once an action plan is in place, appropriate follow-up occurs to check-in with the participant and ensure progress is occurring.

Chapter 4 | Career Coaching Process

The purpose of evidence-based career coaching is to position the individual to take ownership of their career path with the aid of reliable information, processes and tools. Career coaching provides a crucial step for individuals seeking a path to a good job.

The career coach guides participants by helping them (1) interpret their assessment results, (2) explore top career options, (3) make informed decisions, and (4) create a plan of action to pursue a career in their best-fit occupation. These four core components of the coaching process are bookended by preparation and follow-up activities. Throughout, participants may require more or less support depending on their own abilities and readiness. In this chapter, we will describe the typical case, in which individuals require one face-to-face session for each step in the process. The chart on the next page suggests that extensive support might require two sessions per step, and some candidates may only need minimal support by phone or email to accomplish the core activities. Similarly, follow-up activities should be adjusted in accord with how much support each individual participant may need to complete the process.

Career Coaching

Preparation Level	Step 1	Step 2	Step 3	Step 4	Follow-Up Frequency
	Self-Awareness	Option Exploration	Decision Making	Action Plans	
Extensive Support	Individuals may require two face-to-face sessions for each step in the process				Weekly
Typical Support	Individuals likely require one face-to-face session for each step in the process.				Monthly
Minimal Support	Individuals may only require support by phone or email.				Quarterly

What distinguishes "evidence-based" career coaching from standard career coaching processes? In an evidence-based approach, reliable and measurable data provides a foundation for each of the core steps of the career coaching process. Those pieces of information include the following:

- Self-Awareness – Assessment of Career Interests
- Self-Awareness – Assessment of Cognitive Abilities
- Self-Awareness – Assessment of Behavioral Competencies
- Option Exploration – Use of O*NET Data
- Option Exploration – Comparison of interests, skills, and abilities to occupations
- Decision Making – Use of Labor Market Information
- Decision Making – Use of information on available education and training institutions
- Decision Making – Comparison of known resources and barriers to options
- Action Plans – Aligned with above evidence-based decisions

This chapter will provide an overview of the core steps and basic tools that can be used to compete them. We encourage workforce and education partners to include additional tools and supports if necessary.

Coaching Process

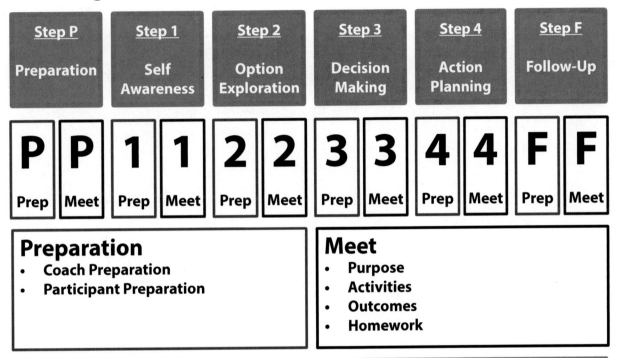

Step P	Step 1	Step 2	Step 3	Step 4	Step F
Preparation	Self Awareness	Option Exploration	Decision Making	Action Planning	Follow-Up

| P Prep | P Meet | 1 Prep | 1 Meet | 2 Prep | 2 Meet | 3 Prep | 3 Meet | 4 Prep | 4 Meet | F Prep | F Meet |

Preparation
- Coach Preparation
- Participant Preparation

Meet
- Purpose
- Activities
- Outcomes
- Homework

How much time is needed?
- The meetings between coach and participant typically total 8 hours (3 hours plus 5 meetings of 1 hour each).
- The preparation times for the coach and participant will vary based on specific needs (5 to 10 hours total each).
- Participants must be willing to spend a few hours on homework assignments between coaching meetings.

Step P - Preparation

Coach Preparation
- Promote the career coaching program
- Provide information and questionnaire
- Review the readiness questionnaire
- Obtain support and approval of supervisor
- Review participant's work and education history

Participant Preparation
- Learn about coaching process and program
- Submit coaching readiness questionnaire
- Submit legal release form
- Submit summary of work and education history

Purpose
Orientation to the career coaching process, review of expectations, and information requirements.

Activities
- Presentation and discussion of expectations, information, and process
- Review example assessment reports
- Administer assessments (O*NET, ETS-DEV, ETS-COG)
- Summarize work and education history

Outcomes
- Confirm clear alignment of expectations
- Assessments completed (O*NET, ETS-DEV, ETS-COG)
- Awareness of the content of assessment reports

Homework
- Create or update resume

How much time and what's between the lines?
- The coach preparation takes 45-90 minutes.
- The participant preparation takes 45-90 minutes.
- The meeting for this step takes 3 hours.
- The preparation for this step occurs via a series of conversations between the coach, participant, participant's supervisor, and appropriate managers.

Step 1 - Self-Awareness

Coach Preparation
- Interpret and analyze score reports
- Review questionnaire for goals and aspirations
- Review work and education history
- Prepare for job families and job codes discussion
- Prepare relevant labor market information (LMI)

Participant Preparation
- Create or update resume

Purpose
Develop a clear and accurate self-understanding via use of assessments, work and education history, and resume.

Activities
- Introduce ETS Career Development Guides for DEV score report
- Interpret score reports (O*NET, ETS-DEV, ETS-WCA)
- Review questionnaire and clarify assumptions
- Introduce labor market information (LMI)
- Introduce Job Family and Job Code charts
- Review resume and provide suggestions

Outcomes
- Self-understanding and insights from assessments
- Awareness of labor market information (LMI)
- Ideas and notes to improve resume

Homework
- Assign the Top Jobs Worksheet exercise (RIASEC)
- Assign the ETS Worksheet exercise
- Assign resume improvement

How much time and what's between the lines?
- The coach preparation takes 45-60 minutes.
- The participant preparation takes 60-90 minutes.
- The meeting for this step takes 45-60 minutes.
- This step guides participants through interpretation and reflection on assessment information to enable a deeper level of introspection and self-understanding.

Step 2 - Option Exploration

Coach Preparation
- Review notes from self-awareness step
- Review assessment score reports, work and education history, and resume
- Reflect on strengths identified by the assessments

Participant Preparation
- Complete the Top Jobs worksheet (including RIASEC)
- Complete ETS Worksheet (reference Career Development Guides)
- Improve resume

Purpose
Begin to create clarity regarding appropriate potential jobs based on the O*NET Interest Profiler and the ETS WorkFORCE assessments.

Activities
- Review Top Jobs Worksheet (O*NET Interest Profiler)
- Review ETS Worksheet and Dev Guides
- Review and interpret labor market information (LMI)
- Review Job Family and Job Code charts
- Summarize collective "strengths" from worksheets

Outcomes
- Clear understanding of potential job opportunities
- Reduce Top Jobs list down to a maximum of three
- Pick a preferred top job for the homework exercise
- Clear awareness of participant's own strengths

Homework
- Assign the JOFI Worksheet exercise
- Assign the Transferable Skills exercise
- Assign ESM Worksheet (education, search, mastery)
- Assign another resume improvement

How much time and what's between the lines?
- The coach preparation takes 45-60 minutes.
- The participant preparation takes 60-90 minutes.
- The meeting for this step takes 45-60 minutes.
- This step includes the critical thinking to clearly understand individual capabilities in the context of evaluating personal job fit to various job opportunities.

Step 3 - Decision Making

Coach Preparation
- Prepare to introduce My Action Plan (MAP)
- Prepare for the ESM Worksheet discussion
- Prepare education and training options
- Prepare work-based learning (WBL) options

Participant Preparation
- Complete the JOFI Worksheet exercise
- Complete the Transferable Skills exercise
- Complete the ESM Worksheet
- Complete another resume improvement

Purpose
Make or confirm the decision for the appropriate target job based on a comprehensive evaluation of options, support needed, and resources available.

Activities
- Review the concept of career pathways
- Clarify choice of education, search, or mastery (ESM)
- Review JOFI Worksheet
- Review Transferable Skills Worksheet
- Compare strengths and credentials to target job
- Review MAP and discuss a potential career path

Outcomes
- Confirm target job, the best next occupation step
- Clarity regarding the choice of education, job search, pursuit of mastery in current role
- Draft Career Pathway MAP (My Action Plan)

Homework
- Assign Career Pathway MAP
- Investigate formal education and training options
- Investigate WBL opportunities
- Assign another resume improvement

How much time and what's between the lines?
- The coach preparation takes 45-90 minutes.
- The participant preparation takes 60-90 minutes.
- The meeting for this step takes 45-60 minutes.
- This step includes the critical thinking and tough choices to move from aspirations to realistic goals considering the current situation, support needed, and resources available

Step 4 - Action Planning

Coach Preparation
- Organize thoughts and notes on formal education and training options
- Organize thoughts and notes on work-based learning opportunities
- Review notes on support needed and available

Participant Preparation
- Complete the Career Pathway MAP
- Organize notes on education and training options
- Organize notes on work-based learning options
- Improve resume

Purpose
Develop and document a plan of actions that will lead through preparation into placement in the target job.

Activities
- Review and improve education and training options
- Review and improve work-based learning options
- Review and improve Career Pathways MAP
- Outline and draft a list of next actions (To Do List)

Outcomes
- Content for final Career Pathway MAP
- List of action items that includes formal education and training items and work-based learning items

Homework
- Document Career Pathway MAP
- Complete and type next actions
- Begin to address some items on the plan

How much time and what's between the lines?
- The coach preparation takes 45-90 minutes.
- The participant preparation takes 60-90 minutes.
- The meeting for this step takes 45-60 minutes.
- This step includes the evaluation of various learning options and the planning to make progress within the constraints of geography, time, and resources.

Step F - Follow-Up

Coach Preparation
- Support progress via conversations with other organizational leaders
- Support progress via conversations with community partners in education and training organizations
- Connect participant to community resources

Participant Preparation
- Document MAP
- Type the plan (action items)
- Update plan as action items change
- Formulate requests for support from coach
- Formulate requests for support from managers

Purpose
Support the participant to achieve each of the next actions in the plan and ultimately to gain employment in the target job.

Activities
- Provide accountability for progress
- Review and record progress on action items
- Discuss barriers and challenges
- Develop strategies to overcome challenges
- Identify specific supports and interventions needed by coach and managers

Outcomes
- Marked up plan (next iteration)
- Placement in target job

Homework
- Iterative revisions to the action plan

How much time and what's between the lines?
- The meetings for this step take 5-20 minutes each.
- This step occurs over a series of phone calls and support meetings to help the participant move forward to achieve their goal of employment in the target job.

How to Use the *Career Pathway MAP: My Action Plan* Form

A central component of the career navigation process is the development of an individualized comprehensive career pathway. Based on nationally-leading work from organizations like the Alliance for Quality Career Pathways (AQCP/CLASP) and the U.S. Department of Labor, the use of career pathways in this process allows individuals to chart the combination of their aspirations and skill sets for long-term career planning.

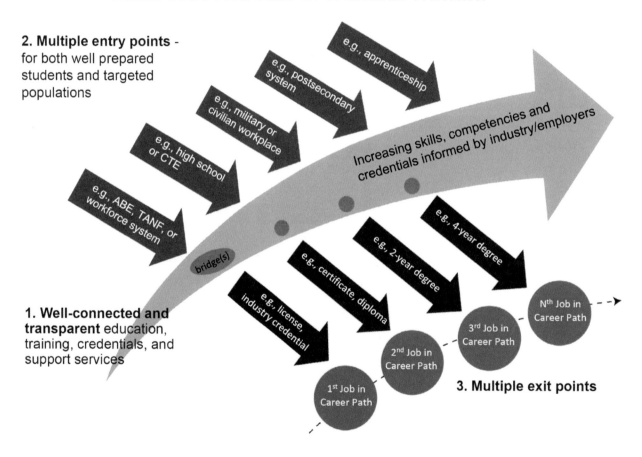

THREE CORE FEATURES OF A CAREER PATHWAY

A comprehensive career pathway contains the following elements, each of which will have been gathered during the four-step career coaching process described above:

- Career Aspirations – an outline of what specific careers an individual seeks to pursue.

- Training & Credential Requirements – an outline of specific training and credentials needed to meet the requirements for stated career aspirations.
- Supportive Services – an outline of the necessary supportive services that will enable an individual's success in securing and maintaining a long-term career.

We suggest that career coaches encourage individuals to document their career pathways through a written narrative using the provided template as part of their career profile. A filled-out template can be used as part of the interview process with employers, just as resumes and cover letters are used. The graphic representation of a career pathway can be a more impactful representation of one's aspirations compared to a written narrative.

When an individual uses the career pathway template (provided on the following page), the following steps should be followed:

- Review career coaching materials to define job families that the individual is interested in pursuing.
- List initial job family/position under Job 1.
- List training programs and relevant credentials that are needed for that job.
- Identify support items that are needed in order to complete the training, receive the credential, and secure and sustain this first job.
- Repeat Steps 2-4 for both Job 2 and Job 3. When filling in information, list the credentials received from the previous job so that by Job 3 the full comprehensive list of credentials has been described within the pathway.

Once the form is filled out, individuals should be able to see and understand the progression of their career plan. In addition, individuals should be able to describe what specific needs they have at the beginning of their pathway, and how those needs can be reduced as they progress through their path. For instance, if transportation is needed for Job 1, individuals should be able to see that progression on this pathway will mean that the issue of transportation needs to be solved by the time they reach Job 2 or Job 3. This form should be informative as well as encouraging for each of the individuals.

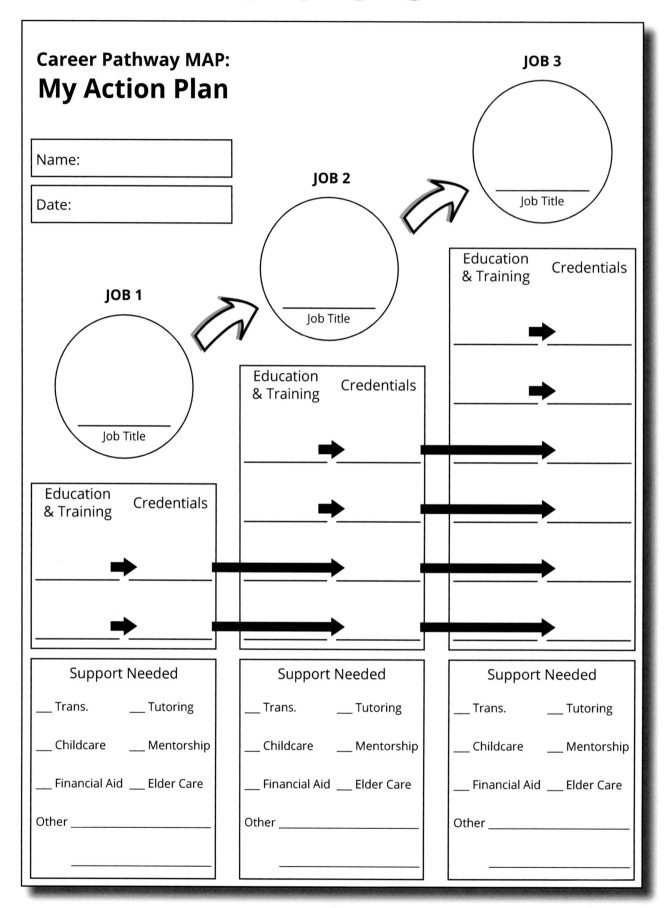

Chapter 5

Career Coaching Tools

Each step in the Career Navigation System described in the last chapter is supported by a set of tools to help participants with each decision as they find path to a good job. The tools consist of worksheets, checklists, and other items.

The tools are numbered sequentially from 1 to 34, and they have also been keyed to the six major process steps:

- (P) Preparation
- (1) Self-Awareness
- (2) Option Exploration
- (3) Decision Making
- (4) Action Planning
- (F) Follow-Up

Steps are therefore numbered P.1, P.2, P.3, 1.1, 1.2, 1.3, etc. to illustrate alignment with the process steps and to help career coaches quickly find the specific tool they need.

For each tool, an image of the tool will appear on the right page and a description of the Purpose, Inputs, Actions and Outcomes will appear on the left page. The explanation are intended to help career coaches answer the following questions:

Purpose:
- Why is this tool included?
- Why do we do this activity?

Inputs:
- What initiates this activity?
- What provides guidance?
- What prerequisites inform the activity?

Activities:
- What steps are to be followed?
- What is the sequence of logic?

Outcomes:
- What is accomplished by this activity?

Like the content in all of the MRI guidebooks, this sequence of tools is offered in the spirit of inspiration, not prescription. We don't expect everyone to use all of the tools, and we encourage experienced practitioners to benchmark their process against our process and tools. We hope that many of them will prove useful and lead to the wider adoption of evidence-based career navigation.

An index of all tools are included on the next page. This list indicates for whom, either the participant, coach, or both, the tool is intended and the page number for reference.

Career Coaching Tools List   **Page**

1. Career Coaching Readiness Questionnaire - Steps P and 1 - Participant...................... 50
2. Work and Education History - Steps P, 1 and 2 - Participant............................... 54
3. Legal Release Form - Step P - Participant... 56
4. Expectations Checklist - Steps P and 1 - Both.. 58
5. Example Report for O*NET Interest Profiler - Step P - Participant....................... 60
6. Example Report for ETS DEV Assessment - Step P - Participant........................... 62
7. Example Report for ETS COG Assessment - Step P - Participant.......................... 64
8. O*NET Interest Profiler - Steps P and 1 - Both... 66
9. ETS Development Assessment - Steps P and 1 - Both..................................... 68
10. ETS Cognitive Assessment - Steps P and 1 - Both....................................... 70
11. Resume - Steps P, 1, 2, 3, 4, and F - Participant.. 72
12. Job Family Chart - Steps 1, 2, and 3 - Both.. 74
13. Job Titles Chart (one per site) - Steps 1, 2, and 3 - Both............................... 76
14. Labor Market Information (LMI) Checklist - Steps 1, 2, and 3 - Both..................... 78
15. ETS Targets for Cognitive Assessment (COG) - Steps 1 and 2 - Both..................... 80
16. ETS Career Development Guides for Assessment (DEV) - Steps 1 and 2 - Both..... 82
17. Interpretation Guide for O*NET Interest Profiler - Steps 1 and 2 - Coach.................. 84
18. Interpretation Guide for ETS DEV (incl. Career Dev Guides) - Steps 1 and 2 - Coach.. 86
19. Interpretation Guide for ETS Cognitive - Steps 1 and 2 - Coach......................... 88
20. Probing Questions for Assessment Debriefs - Step 1 - Coach........................... 90
21. Resume Checklist - Steps 1, 2, 3, and 4 - Coach....................................... 92
22. Top Jobs (RIASEC) Worksheet - Steps 1 and 2 - Participant............................ 94
23. ETS Assessments Worksheet - Steps 1 and 2 - Participant............................. 96
24. Strengths Summary Worksheet - Steps 2 and 3 - Participant............................ 98
25. Growth Opportunities Worksheet - Steps 2, 3, and 4 - Participant...................... 100
26. Option Exploration Questions - Step 2 - Coach... 102
27. JOFI Skills Worksheet - Steps 2 and 3 - Participant.................................... 104
28. Transferable Skills Worksheet - Steps 2 and 3 - Participant............................ 106
29. ESM Worksheet (Education, Search, or Mastery Path) - Steps 2 and 3 - Participant.. 108
30. Career Pathways Concept Discussion Checklist - Steps 3 and 4 - Both................. 110
31. Career Pathway MAP (My Action Plan) - Steps 3 and 4 - Participant.................... 112
32. Decision Making Checklist - Steps 3 and 4 - Participant................................ 114
33. Learning Options Worksheet - Steps 3 and 4 - Participant.............................. 116
34. To Do List of Next Actions - Steps 4 and F - Participant................................ 118

Tool 1 - Step P.1
Coaching Readiness Questionnaire

Purpose
- The career coaching readiness questionnaire helps the potential participant and coaching program staff determine if the participant is ready for the career coaching process.
- The use of the form as part of the application process is a method to enable the potential participant to self-select in or out of the program.

Inputs
- Participant responds to program promotion and asks for more information
- Coach or administrator provides the form

Activities
- Participant fills out the questionnaire
- Participant has the opportunity to reflect on career aspirations while answering questions

Outcomes
- If the participant is ready, they will take the time to thoughtfully fill out the form completely
- If the participant is not ready, they will likely not take the time to fill out the form and not turn it in

Tool 1 - Step P.1
Coaching Readiness Questionnaire

Referral Agency _____   Date _____

Last Name _____   First Name _____   MI _____

Address _____   _____

City _____   State _____   Zip _____

Home Phone _____   Cell Phone _____

Email _____

1. Which of these growth industries are you most interested in?

☐ Health Care   ☐ Advanced Manufacturing   ☐ Information Technology

☐ Life Sciences   ☐ Energy   ☐ Other _____

2. What type of assignment are you most interested in?

☐ Assembly   ☐ Office/Clerical   ☐ Warehouse   ☐ Machine Op   ☐ Managerial

☐ Training/HR   ☐ Quality   ☐ Inventory   ☐ Other_____

3. What specific career are you considering?
   What has influenced you?

4. Do you know someone who is currently working in this career? If yes, describe what they do.

5. How do you see yourself growing in the profession?

6. Describe any work experience that you have in this profession and what is was like for you.

7. What are 3 reasons you think you would really enjoy working in this profession?	What are 3 things you think you would like least about working in this profession?

8. Would you consider starting in an entry-level position? ☐ Yes ☐ No

9. Do you have reliable transportation? ☐ Yes ☐ No

   If yes, how will you get to work? ☐ Own car ☐ Bus ☐ Car pool ☐ Bicycle ☐ Walk ☐ Taxi

10. Do you enjoy working with and helping others? Why or why not?

Tool 1 - Step P.1
Coaching Readiness Questionnaire

11. Describe a time when you were part of a team; what was your role and contribution?

12. Describe a time when you were responsible for coordinating something that involved either people and/or tasks.

13. Describe a situation where you had to keep something confidential.

14. On a scale of 1-10, what is your skill and comfort level with computers and technology?

    Low   High

    0   1   2   3   4   5   6   7   8   9   10

14. Describe your Education:

    High school diploma or GED ☐ Yes ☐ No - Expected date of completion _____
    Trade or Vocational Classes, Certificates or Licenses _____
    ☐ Some College ☐ Associate ☐ Bachelor ☐ Master

    Number of Credit Hours _____ Course of Study _____
    Have you taken the WorkKeys tests? ☐ Yes ☐ No
    If yes, do you have the WorkKeys National Career Readiness Certificate? ☐ Yes ☐ No
    If yes, what level have you achieved? ☐ Bronze ☐ Silver ☐ Gold ☐ Platinum
    If no, would you be willing to obtain a National Career Readiness Certificate? ☐ Yes ☐ No

14. If needed as a responsibility of employment, are you able to lift 30 pounds? ☐ Yes ☐ No

15. Have you ever been disciplined or released from a job due to poor attendance or job performance issues? ☐ No ☐ Yes If yes, explain fully each event including the date, facts presented by employer, and explanation of actions you took to resolve the issue.

16. Many careers typically require pre-employment, reasonable cause, and random drug tests. Please indicate if this is a problem for you. ☐ No ☐ Yes If yes, why?

17. Have you ever been convicted of or pled guilty or not contest to a criminal offense? ☐ No ☐ Yes
    If yes, please indicate the date and nature of each offense. (Please include any conviction other than minor traffic offenses such as those carrying fines of less than $100 or two points. For purposes of this question, a plea of 'nolo contendre' or 'no contest' constitutes a conviction.) Note that answering yes to this question will not necessarily disqualify you from employment, but any omission or misstatement will disqualify you from consideration from employment.

Thank you for completing this questionnaire.
This service is designed to enhance your career decision making process.
Below is additional information important to making this program successful for you.

PLEASE TAKE THIS SHEET WITH YOU

1. If you have not already done so, please schedule a time to take your WorkKeys assessments. **Your assessment results are required before your first session with the Career Coach.**

2. Once everything above is complete and the questionnaire is reviewed you will be contacted to confirm the following schedule which occurs over a three week period:

Career Coaching Session 1	3 Hours	Take PSA test

Additional sessions will be scheduled with the Career Coach:

Career Coaching Session 2	½ hour (same week)	Review assessments and identify 3 best fit occupations
Career Coaching Session 3	½ hour (following week)	Identify one best fit occupational target
Career Coaching Session 4	½ hour, any day following week	Present education and/or career plan

It is important to note that there are homework assignments that must be completed in between sessions.

We hope you enjoy your journey through the career coaching process.
Please contact us if you have any questions.

Tool 2 - Step P.2
Work and Education History

Purpose
- The work and education history is a first step toward preparing a complete and accurate resume.
- This is an easier step because it asks only for content in two areas and avoids concerns about format.

Inputs
- Participant reflects and records education history
- Participant reflects and records work history

Activities
- Write a comprehensive list of education and training
- Write a comprehensive list of jobs

Outcomes
- A comprehensive chronological list of the participants work and education history

Tool 2 - Step P.2
Work and Education History

Work and Education History	
Take a few moments to reflect on your work history. Record your work experiences here.	

	Organization	Job
Work History		

Reflect on your education history and record your educational experiences here.

	Institution	Program
Education History		

Tool 3 - Step P.3
Legal Release and Authorization Form

Purpose
- The legal release provides the coach and the host organization permission to share information with appropriate community partners.
- This supports the ability to provide the participant development feedback from various sources.
- This supports the ability to improve community collaboration and the career coaching program.

Inputs
- Coach or administrator provide the release form

Activities
- Participant carefully reviews the form
- Questions, if any, are answered
- Participant signs and returns the form

Outcomes
- Properly executed legal release and authorization form is filed at the host organization

RELEASE AND AUTHORIZATION

I, _____, hereby authorize Mercy Health Partners, Trinity Health-
      (Print Participant's Name)

Michigan d/b/a Mercy Health Saint Mary's, and Advantage Health/Saint Mary's Medical Group d/b/a

Mercy Health Physician Partners (collectively "Mercy Health"), Mercy Health's parent corporation Trinity

Health Inc., its member organizations, corporations and assigns, acting through their authorized employees or

agents and in their discretion, to provide any information it has at its disposal to the West Michigan Works!

(WMW) relative to my activities at Mercy Health as part of the Career Pathways Program. I hereby release and

hold harmless Mercy Health and Trinity Health, Inc., from any liability associated with the provision of

information, whether from documents from its files or from the verbal provision of any personal judgments,

impressions, evaluations or opinions relative to any of my activities including training, experience, supportive

services, placement needs and employment goals. I understand also that information reported by Mercy Health

to Career Pathways Program may include information on my program participation, including my status and

outcomes, and provide feedback for career coaching. I understand that my participation in the Career Pathways

Program does not guarantee employment with Mercy Health, nor would it exclude employment with Mercy

Health. I hereby waive any claims associated with Mercy Health release of information or Mercy Health's

decision to employ/not employ me; including, but not limited to, claims based on discrimination, libel, slander

or related claims or causes of action of any kind.

    I sign this Release and Authorization to Provide Information knowingly and freely without any

promises, duress or threat of any kind.

Signed,

_____   _____   _____
Participant Signature   Printed Name   Date

_____   _____   _____
Witness Signature   Printed Name   Date

Tool 4 - Step P.4
Expectations Checklist

Purpose
- The expectations checklist provides a guide for a frank conversation between the coach and participant to ensure clarity around the expectations of the participant throughout the coaching process.

Inputs
- Coach provides the checklist

Activities
- Coach reviews the checklist and prepares for discussion with the participant
- Coach reviews the checklist items with the participant
- Dialog to lead to a common understanding of expectations

Outcomes
- Participant has a clear understanding of expectations
- Participant expresses commitment to meet expectations to the coach

Expectations Checklist

The coaching participant has the primary responsibility to manage progress through the process. The coach, like in sports, will be on the sidelines supporting and guiding. The participant is on the field responsible for moving the ball forward.

Participants are expected to demonstrate the following characteristics throughout the process:

- Initiative - a willingness to take on responsibilities and challenges.

- Persistence - persistence in the face of obstacles.

- Cooperation - being pleasant with others on the job and displaying a good-natured, cooperative attitude.

- Self-Control - maintaining composure, keeping emotions in check, controlling anger, and avoiding aggressive behavior, even in very difficult situations.

- Dependability - being reliable, responsible, and dependable, and fulfilling obligations.

- Analytical Thinking - analyzing information and using logic to address work-related issues and problems.

Roles:

- Participant - The coaching participant has the primary responsibility to advance through the process in a timely manner. Participants are expected to make and keep appointments with the coach and are expected to devote appropriate time to homework between sessions. Transportation issues must be planned and managed with professionalism.

- Coach - The coach is primarily a facilitator of the process. The coach will teach the process to the participant and set up assignments to enable the participant to be successful.

Tool 5 - Step P.5
Example Report O*NET Interest Profiler

Purpose
- The example O*NET Interest Profiler report enables the participant to become familiar with the tool prior to taking the on-line survey.
- This enables the participant to focus on understanding the content and purpose of the report rather than on their results.

Inputs
- The coach or administrator provides an example report to the participant

Activities
- Review the Interest Profiler report
- Discuss answers to questions about the rating scales, RIASEC model, job zones, and occupational titles

Outcomes
- Participant familiarity with the Interest Profiler

Tool 5 - Step P.5
Example Report O*NET Interest Profiler

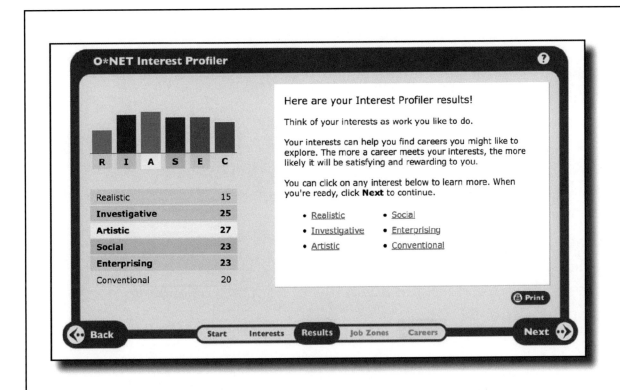

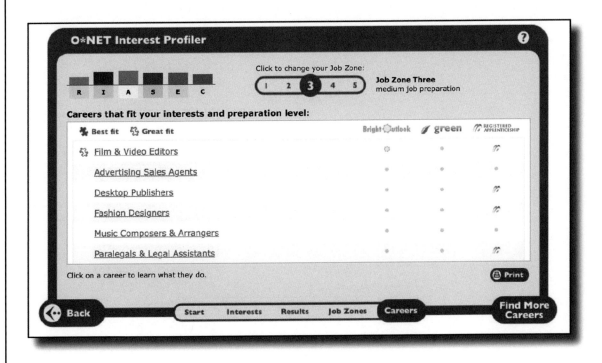

Tool 6 - Step P.6
Example Report ETS DEV Assessment

Purpose
- The example ETS Development assessment report enables the participant to become familiar with the tool prior to taking the on-line assessment.
- This enables the participant to focus on understanding the content and purpose of the assessment rather than on their results.

Inputs
- The coach or administrator provides an example report to the participant

Activities
- Review the ETS Development report
- Discuss answers to questions about the rating scales, behavioral competencies, and facets

Outcomes
- Participant familiarity with the ETS Development assessment

Tool 6 - Step P.6
Example Report ETS DEV Assessment

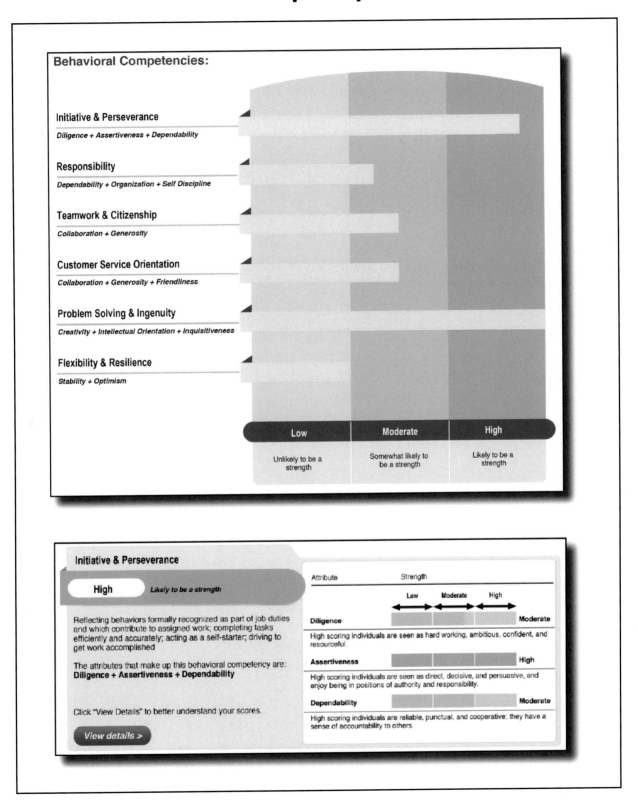

Tool 7 - Step P.7
Example Report ETS COG Assessment

Purpose
- The example ETS Cognitive assessment report enables the participant to become familiar with the tool prior to taking the on-line assessment.
- This enables the participant to focus on understanding the content and purpose of the assessment rather than on their results.

Inputs
- The coach or administrator provides an example report to the participant

Activities
- Review the ETS Cognitive report
- Discuss answers to questions about the rating scales and cognitive competencies

Outcomes
- Participant familiarity with the ETS Cognitive assessment

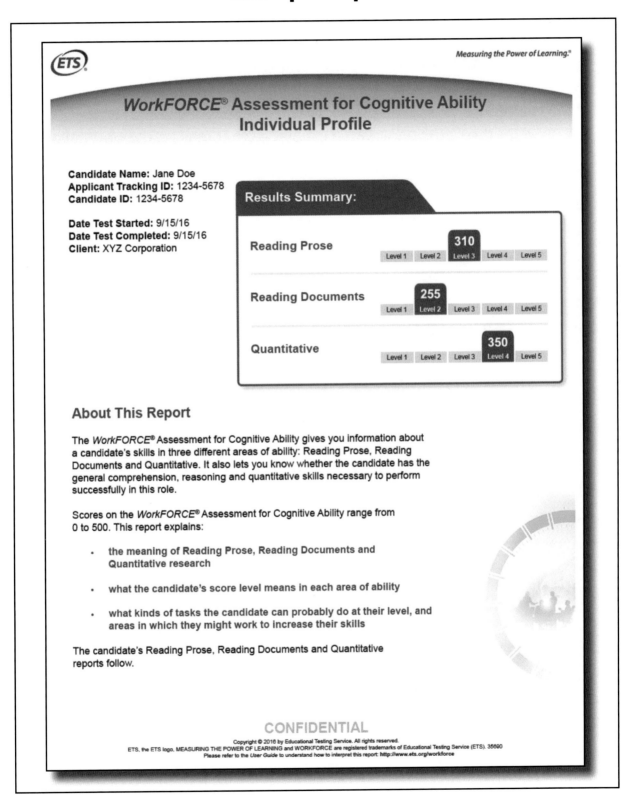

(ETS) — *Measuring the Power of Learning.*

WorkFORCE® Assessment for Cognitive Ability
Individual Profile

Candidate Name: Jane Doe
Applicant Tracking ID: 1234-5678
Candidate ID: 1234-5678

Date Test Started: 9/15/16
Date Test Completed: 9/15/16
Client: XYZ Corporation

Results Summary:

Reading Prose	**310** — Level 1 / Level 2 / Level 3 / Level 4 / Level 5
Reading Documents	**255** — Level 1 / Level 2 / Level 3 / Level 4 / Level 5
Quantitative	**350** — Level 1 / Level 2 / Level 3 / Level 4 / Level 5

About This Report

The *WorkFORCE®* Assessment for Cognitive Ability gives you information about a candidate's skills in three different areas of ability: Reading Prose, Reading Documents and Quantitative. It also lets you know whether the candidate has the general comprehension, reasoning and quantitative skills necessary to perform successfully in this role.

Scores on the *WorkFORCE®* Assessment for Cognitive Ability range from 0 to 500. This report explains:

- the meaning of Reading Prose, Reading Documents and Quantitative research

- what the candidate's score level means in each area of ability

- what kinds of tasks the candidate can probably do at their level, and areas in which they might work to increase their skills

The candidate's Reading Prose, Reading Documents and Quantitative reports follow.

Tool 8 - Step P.8
O*NET Interest Profiler

Purpose
- The O*NET Interest Profiler enables the participant to become familiar with occupational titles that are a potential good fit based on their career interests.
- This provides the participant with a list of jobs that may be the optimal next step in their career path.

Inputs
- The coach or administrator asks the participant to complete the interest assessment at https://www.mynextmove.org/explore/ip

Activities
- Start Interest Profiler
- Answer all questions
- Review RIASEC profile
- Select an appropriate job zone
- Review potential jobs (occupational titles)
- Optional: Download and take the CIP (long-form) from https://www.onetcenter.org/IP.html?p=5

Outcomes
- RIASEC Profile
- List of occupational titles that are a good fit based on interests

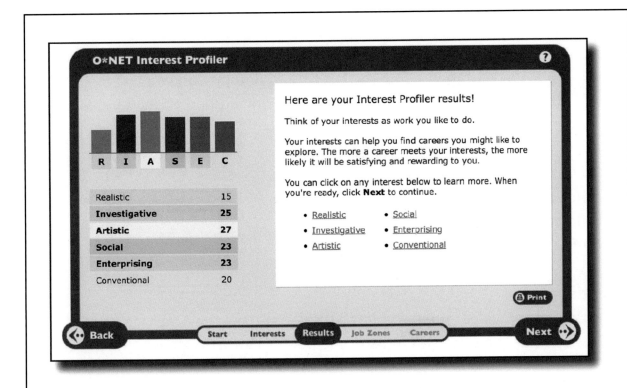

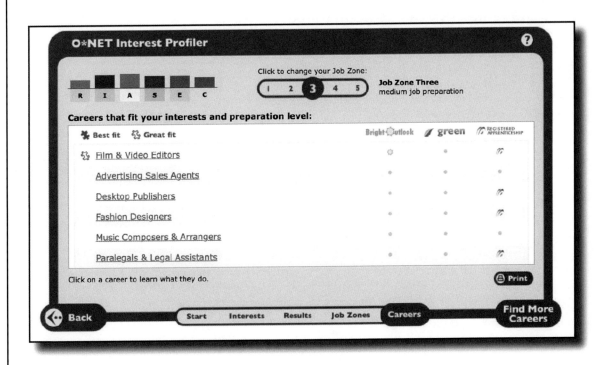

Tool 9 - Step P.9
ETS Development Assessment

Purpose
- The ETS Development assessment enables the participant to learn about their behavioral competencies and the underlying personality facets.
- This is the behavioral (personality) portion of developing an evidence-based self-awareness.

Inputs
- Participant's government issued photo ID
- Participant's email address
- The ETMS test management system

Activities
- Participant provides a government issued photo ID
- The coach or administrator register the participant with legal name in the ETMS registration system
- The link and password are emailed to the participant
- Participant completes the assessment (30 minutes)
- The assessment results are emailed to the participant

Outcomes
- Six behavioral competency scales and ratings
- Thirteen supporting facet scales and ratings

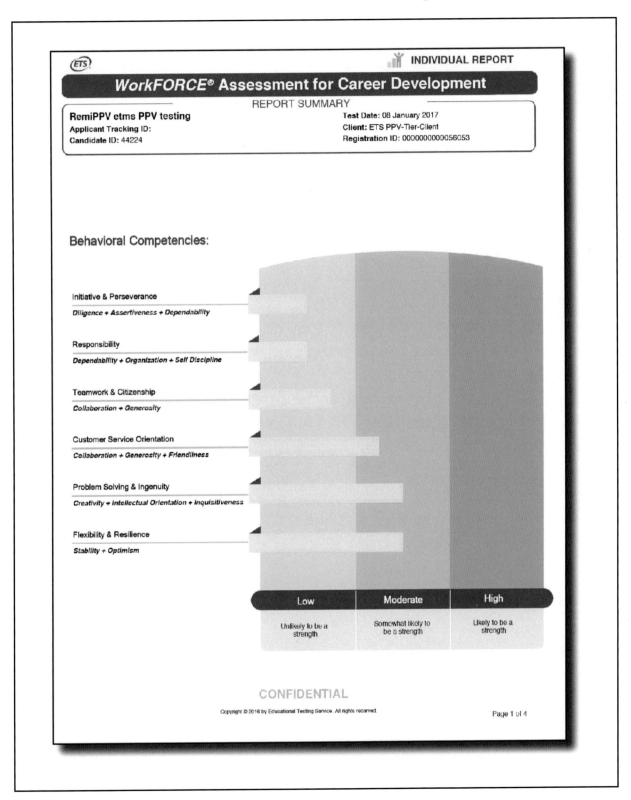

(ETS)   **INDIVIDUAL REPORT**

WorkFORCE® Assessment for Career Development

REPORT SUMMARY

RemiPPV etms PPV testing
Applicant Tracking ID:
Candidate ID: 44224

Test Date: 08 January 2017
Client: ETS PPV-Tier-Client
Registration ID: 0000000000056053

Behavioral Competencies:

Initiative & Perseverance
Diligence + Assertiveness + Dependability

Responsibility
Dependability + Organization + Self Discipline

Teamwork & Citizenship
Collaboration + Generosity

Customer Service Orientation
Collaboration + Generosity + Friendliness

Problem Solving & Ingenuity
Creativity + Intellectual Orientation + Inquisitiveness

Flexibility & Resilience
Stability + Optimism

Low	Moderate	High
Unlikely to be a strength	Somewhat likely to be a strength	Likely to be a strength

Page 1 of 4

Tool 10 - Step P.10
ETS Cognitive Assessment

Purpose
- The ETS Cognitive assessment enables the participant to learn about their cognitive competencies (Prose, Document, and Quantitative).
- This is the cognitive portion of developing an evidence-based self-awareness.

Inputs
- Participant's government issued photo ID
- Participant's email address
- The ETMS test management system

Activities
- Participant provides a government issued photo ID
- The coach or administrator register the participant with legal name in the ETMS registration system
- The link and password are emailed to the participant
- Participant completes the assessment (90 minutes)
- The assessment results are emailed to the participant

Outcomes
- Three cognitive competency scales and ratings: Reading Prose, Reading Documents, & Quantitative

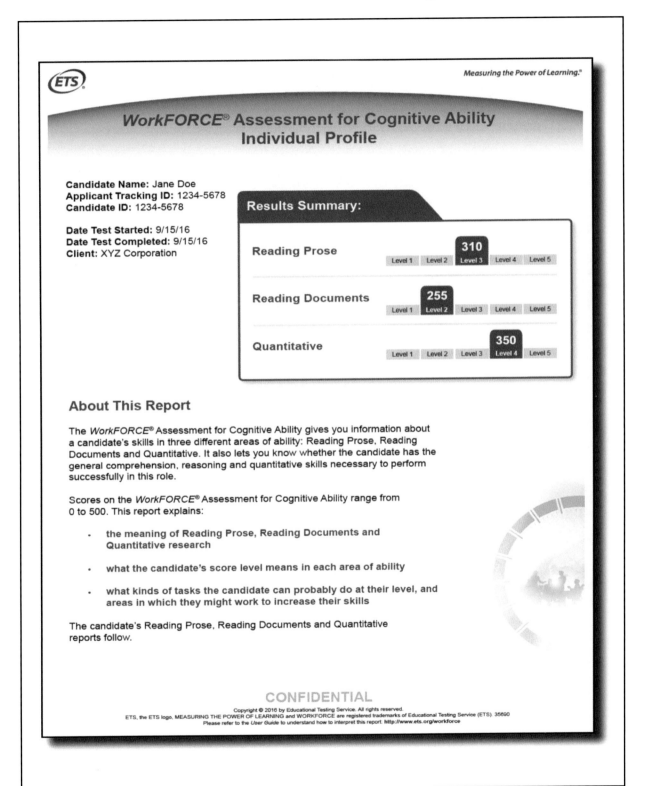

Candidate Name: Jane Doe
Applicant Tracking ID: 1234-5678
Candidate ID: 1234-5678

Date Test Started: 9/15/16
Date Test Completed: 9/15/16
Client: XYZ Corporation

WorkFORCE® Assessment for Cognitive Ability
Individual Profile

Results Summary:

Area	Score	Level
Reading Prose	310	Level 3
Reading Documents	255	Level 2
Quantitative	350	Level 4

About This Report

The WorkFORCE® Assessment for Cognitive Ability gives you information about a candidate's skills in three different areas of ability: Reading Prose, Reading Documents and Quantitative. It also lets you know whether the candidate has the general comprehension, reasoning and quantitative skills necessary to perform successfully in this role.

Scores on the WorkFORCE® Assessment for Cognitive Ability range from 0 to 500. This report explains:

- the meaning of Reading Prose, Reading Documents and Quantitative research
- what the candidate's score level means in each area of ability
- what kinds of tasks the candidate can probably do at their level, and areas in which they might work to increase their skills

The candidate's Reading Prose, Reading Documents and Quantitative reports follow.

Tool 11 - Step P.11
Resume

Purpose
- The resume is an essential communication tool that is required for the job search process. On-line application systems ask for content that is typically found on resumes and many allow applicants to upload resumes into the system.
- Resume development via an iterative process provides the opportunity for critical thinking to organize key points clearly and concisely.

Inputs
- The resume is first assigned as homework in the preparation step
- The work and education history has content that is helpful for the initial resume

Activities
- The resume is developed iteratively at each step
- Each iteration requires participant reflection
- Each iteration benefits from coach input

Outcomes
- A high quality resume that is useful to support job search and placement activities

Resume Template

3456 SE 123 Ave. West Miami, FL 15677
Home (305) 555-4554   Cell# (786) 555-0097

EXPERIENCE:

2/98 – Present	**Lifetime Accounting**	Coral Gables, FL

Accountant:
- Keeps, audits and inspects financial records of business
- Prepares financial and tax reports
- Partners with different departments to increase efficiency

6/90-2/98	**Taxing Company**	West Palm Beach, FL

Jr. Accountant:
- Processed vendor invoices and check requests for payment
- Maintained records of accounts payable, invoice register, cash disbursement journal and cash advance log
- Prepared accounting analysis as needed

2/86-4/90	**Jones Corporation**	Miami, FL

A/P Coordinator:
- Responsible for processing vendor invoices
- Prepared reports at the direction of the A/P Manager

EDUCATION: University of Miami
Bachelors of Science in Accounting (May 1990)
Graduated Summa Cum Lade
CPA

SKILLS:

- English and Spanish (Verbal and written)
- Part time professor at Miami Dade Community College
- Proficient in Microsoft Suite
- Expert on Tax Law

REFERENCES: Available upon request

Tool 12 - Step 1.1
Job Family Chart

Purpose
- Job families illustrate the structure of jobs in the jobs market within each industry sector.
- Job families provide a framework to more deeply understand work history and to plan job progression.
- Job families provide a framework to organize and analyze job requirements, including skills and credentials, related to job performance.

Inputs
- The coach provides a copy of the relevant job families chart and provides an introduction and overview

Activities
- Carefully review the job family chart
- Identify job families related to work history
- Identify job families related to job aspirations

Outcomes
- Participant has a framework to understand the sea of jobs and job opportunities open to them
- Participant has a framework for organizing skills and credentials related to jobs

Tool 12 - Step 1.1
Job Family Chart

Job Zone	Job Family	GoodPaths Job Family	#	ONET Code	ONET Occupation Title	Example NRSI and Goodwill Job Titles	
		GoodPaths Retail Job Families				**Rev: 2017-05-12**	
		GoodPaths Job Family	#	ONET Code	ONET Occupation Title	Example NRSI and Goodwill Job Titles	
				Job Zone 1 - Little or No Preparation Needed - Entry-Level Jobs			
Z1	1	Food Preparation Zn1	1	35-2011.00	Cooks, Fast Food	Cook	
Z1	1	Food Preparation Zn1	2	35-2015.00	Cooks, Short Order	Cook	
Z1	1	Food Preparation Zn1	3	35-2021.00	Food Preparation Workers	Food Preparer	
Z1	1	Food Preparation Zn1	4	35-3021.00	Combined Food Preparation and Serving Workers, Including Fast Food		
Z1	1	Food Preparation Zn1	5	51-3022.00	Meat, Poultry, and Fish Cutters and Trimmers		
Z1	2	Food Service Zn1	6	35-3022.00	Counter Attendants, Cafeteria, Food Concession, and Coffee Shop		
Z1	2	Food Service Zn1	7	35-3022.01	Baristas		
Z1	2	Food Service Zn1	8	35-3031.00	Waiters and Waitresses		
Z1	2	Food Service Zn1	9	35-3041.00	Food Servers, Nonrestaurant	Server	
Z1	2	Food Service Zn1	10	35-9011.00	Dining Room and Cafeteria Attendants and Bartender Helpers	Busser	
Z1	2	Food Service Zn1	11	35-9031.00	Hosts and Hostesses, Restaurant, Lounge, and Coffee Shop	Host	
Z1	3	Clerks Zn1	12	41-2011.00	Cashiers	Cashier	Cashier
Z1	3	Clerks Zn1	13	41-2021.00	Counter and Rental Clerks	Front Desk Associate	
Z1	4	Washers and Cleaners	14	51-6011.00	Laundry and Dry-Cleaning Workers		
Z1	4	Washers and Cleaners	15	51-6021.00	Pressers, Textile, Garment, and Related Materials		
Z1	4	Washers and Cleaners	16	35-9021.00	Dishwashers	Dishwasher	
				Job Zone 2 - Some Preparation Needed - Next-Level Jobs			
Z2	5	Clerks Zn2	1	43-3021.02	Billing, Cost and Rate Clerks	Billing Clerk	
Z2	5	Clerks Zn2	2	43-4051.00	Customer Service Representatives	Customer Service Agent	
Z2	5	Clerks Zn2	3	43-9021.00	Data Entry Keyer	Data Entry Operator	
Z2	5	Clerks Zn2	4	43-9061.00	Office Clerks, General	Administrative Clerk	
Z2	5	Clerks Zn2	5	43-4151.00	Order Clerks	Process Operator	
Z2	5	Clerks Zn2	6	43-5011.00	Cargo and Freight Agents	Logistics	
Z2	5	Clerks Zn2	7	43-3051.00	Payroll and Timekeeping Clerks	Help Desk Associate	
Z2	5	Clerks Zn2	8	43-3021.01	Statement Clerks	Billing Clerks	
Z2	6	Drivers	9	53-3031.00	Driver/Sales Workers	Driver	Truck Driver / Driver Helper
Z2	6	Drivers	10	53-7051.00	Industrial Truck and Tractor Operators	Fork Lift Operator	Forklift Operator
Z2	6	Drivers	11	53-3033.00	Light Truck or Delivery Services Drivers	Driver	Driver, Lead Driver
Z2	6	Drivers	12	53-7081.00	Refuse and Recyclable Material Collectors		
Z2	7	Environmental Services Zn2	13	53-7061.00	Cleaners of Vehicles and Equipment		
Z2	7	Environmental Services Zn2	14	37-2011.00	Janitors and Cleaners, Except Maids and Housekeeping Cleaners		
Z2	7	Environmental Services Zn2	15	37-2012.00	Maids and Housekeeping Cleaners	Housekeeper	Housekeeper, Janitor

Summary List of Job Families and Job Titles

Zone	#		
Zone 1	1	Food Preparation Zn1	Cooks, Food Preparation Workers, Meat and Fish Trimers
	2	Food Service Zn1	Cafeteria, Concession, Coffee Shop, Baristas, Waiters, Waiters, Hosts
	3	Clerk Zn1	Cashiers, Counter and Rental Clerks
	4	Washers Cleaners	Laundry, Dry-Cleaning, Pressers, Textile, Garment, Dishwashers
Zone 2	5	Clerk Zn2	Customer Service, Billing, Marking, Office, Order, Payroll, Shipping, Stock
	6	Drivers	Drivers, Industrial Truck Operators, Delivery Services
	7	Environmental Services	Cleaners of Vehicles, Janitors and Cleaners, Maids and Housekeepers
	8	Food Preparation Zn2	Bakers, Butchers, Cooks, Roasting, Drying, Batchmakers, Bartenders
	9	Maintenance Repair Zn2	Auto, Watercraft, Bicycle, Outdoor Power Equipment, Tire, and Shoe
	10	Operators	Office Machines, Photographic Machines, Switchboard, and Telephone
	11	Production	Recycling, Reclamation, Collectors, Inspectors, Testers, Sorters, Packers
	12	Sales	Demonstrate, Promote, Parts, Pharmacy
	13	Security	Security Guards and Retail Loss Prevention Specialists
	14	Stock Logistics	Freight Stock, Material Movers, Order Fillers
	15	Supervisors Zn2	Food, Helpers, Labor, Material Movers, Housekeeping, Production, Sales
Zone 3	16	Clerks Zn3	Bookkeeping, Procurement, Production Planning, Executive Assistants
	17	Food Preparation Zn3	Chefs, Head Cooks, Private Cooks
	18	Maintenance Repair Zn3	Computer, Office Machine, Electronics, Automotive, Motorcycle, Appliance
	19	Managers Zn3	Administrative Services, Food Services
	20	Professionals Zn3	Buyers, Credit, Sales, Human Resources
	21	Supervisors Zn3	Office and Administrative, Mechanics, Installers, Repairers
	22	Technicians	Computer, Quality, Display, Audio Video, Pharmacy, Optician, Electronic, Tailors, Jewelers
Zone 4	23	Managers Zn4	Advertising, Compensation, Computers, Marketing, Purchasing, Supply Chain
	24	Professionals Zn4	Accountants, Buyers, Compensation, Fraud, Information, Logistics, Marketing, Software, Development
Zone 5	25	Executives	Chief Executives
	26	Professionals Zn5	Audiologists, Economists, Management Analysts, Dietitians, Nutritionists, Optometrists, Pharmacists

Tool 13 - Step 1.2
Job Titles Chart

Purpose
- The job titles chart connects local job titles in specific organizations to job families.
- The job titles chart contextualizes the job families so that participants can relate local jobs to the jobs in the job family chart.

Inputs
- The coach provides a copy of the relevant job titles chart and provides an introduction and overview

Activities
- Introduce and carefully review the job titles chart
- Identify job titles related to work history
- Identify job titles related to job aspirations
- Dialog to discuss how the job families chart and job titles chart work together frame the jobs and job requirements in the sector and organization

Outcomes
- Participant understands how the job families chart is helpful to identify job requirements for various job opportunities
- Participant understands how the job titles chart is a cross-walk from local job titles to job families

JF#	Job Family Title	Job Title	Division	Required Education/Licensing/Experience
2	Food Service Zn1	Food Service Worker (Box Lunch)	Contracts	Prefer one (1) year experience in high volume food service operation.
2	Food Service Zn1	Food Service Worker	Contracts	Prefer one (1) year experience in high volume food service operation.
3	Clerk Zn1	Cashier	Retail	High school diploma or GED and 1 year experience as a cashier (preferred).
3	Clerk Zn1	PC Store Associate	Retail	There is no educational or experience qualifications for this position.
3	Clerk Zn1	Stock Clerk	Contracts	No specified educational requirements. Must have the ability to read and write English and perform simple math (addition and subtraction).
3	Clerk Zn1	Store Associate II	Retail	No specific educational or experience qualifications for this position.
3	Clerk Zn1	Store Associate	Retail	No specific educational or experience qualifications for this position.
3	Clerk Zn1	Store Worker I	Contracts	No specified educational requirements except an ability to read numbers and distinguish between sizes, shapes and to match like items. Prior stocking experience is preferred.
5	Clerk Zn2	General Clerk I (393)	Contracts	High school diploma or equivalent. Experience in working with disabled individuals preferred. Data entry skills required Experience in a military installation (preferred).
5	Clerk Zn2	General Clerk I (395)	Contracts	High school diploma or equivalent. Experience in working with disabled individuals preferred. Data entry skills (preferred). Experience in a military installation (preferred).
5	Clerk Zn2	General Clerk II (397)	Contracts	High school diploma or equivalent. Experience in working with disabled individuals preferred. Data entry skills (preferred). Experience in a military installation (preferred).
5	Clerk Zn2	General Clerk III (392/399)	Contracts	High School Graduate or GED. Some college preferred but not required. Two to five years as a full duty secretary or Administrative Assistant is preferred
6	Drivers	Tractor Trailer Driver	Warehouse	No formal education required. One year experience as a combination tractor trailer driver or successful completion of tractor trailer school. Must possess a valid driver's license, (Class A; CDL). Must be DOT Certified
6	Drivers	Truck Driver	Warehouse	No formal education required.
7	Environmental Services	Janitor	Contracts	High school diploma or General Education Degree (GED) preferred
8	Food Preparation Zn2	Cook I	Contracts	High school graduate. One (1) year experience volume food preparation.
8	Food Preparation Zn2	Cook II	Contracts	Five (5) years' experience in volume food preparation. Experience in a supervisor position preferred
9	Maintenance Repair Zn2	Day Porter	Facilities Maintenance	High school diploma or General Education Degree (GED) preferred.
9	Maintenance Repair Zn2	Facilities Maintenance Engineer I	Facilities Maintenance	High school diploma or general education degree (GED) and two years' experience providing maintenance services to include plumbing and construction, or equivalent combination of education and experience.
9	Maintenance Repair Zn2	Floor Care and General Maintenance Tech	Facilities Maintenance	High school diploma or General Education Degree (GED) preferred.
11	Production	Baler	Retail	Able to operate baling machine. Able to operate counter-balance scale to weigh bales.
12	Sales	E-Commerce Specialist I	Retail	High school diploma or equivalent. Experience in working with disabled individuals preferred. Data entry skills required.
12	Sales	E-Commerce Specialist II	Retail	High school diploma or equivalent. Experience in working with disabled individuals preferred. Data entry skills required
12	Sales	Shop Goodwill Specialist	Retail	High school diploma or equivalent. Experience in working with disabled individuals preferred. Data entry skills required.
14	Stock Logistics	Shop Goodwill Shipping Specialist	Retail	High school diploma or equivalent. Experience in working with disabled individuals preferred. Data entry skills required.
14	Stock Logistics	Warehouse Worker	Warehouse	No specific educational levels are required. Must be able to read and write.
15	Supervisors Zn2	APM Commissary	Contracts	Must have high school diploma or equivalent. Must have two years of experience in contract or related experience in shelf stocking, order writing, warehousing and custodial. Experience in working with disabled individuals preferred.
15	Supervisors Zn2	APM Custodial	Contracts	Must have high school diploma or equivalent. Must have two years' experience in custodial or related supervisory experience. Experience in working with disabled individuals preferred.
15	Supervisors Zn2	APM Food Service	Contracts	High school diploma or equivalent. Previous experience of two years food service operations
15	Supervisors Zn2	Custodial Supervisor	Contracts	Two years supervisory experience in all phases of custodial operations. Experience in working with disabled individuals preferred.
15	Supervisors Zn2	Dining Room Supervisor	Contracts	Experience in working with disabled individuals preferred. Experience in a military installation. High school diploma, some college preferred. Five (5) years' experience in volume food preparation.
15	Supervisors Zn2	Job Coach	Mission Services	Minimum of a high school diploma or its equivalent. An awareness of and experience in training disabled individuals. Knowledge of competitive employment work environments, policies and procedures
15	Supervisors Zn2	Lead Food Service Worker (391)	Contracts	Prefer one (1) year experience in volume food service operation.
15	Supervisors Zn2	Lead Janitor	Contracts	High school diploma or General Education Degree (GED) preferred
15	Supervisors Zn2	Lead Store Associate	Retail	High School diplomas or general education degree (GED) and one year of retail experience; or equivalent combination of education and experience.

Tool 14 - Step 1.3
Labor Market Information Checklist

Purpose
- The LMI checklist creates awareness of the availability of labor market information.
- The checklist ensures that the participant becomes aware of the local information that could be helpful in their career planning and navigation.

Inputs
- The coach provides the labor market information (LMI) checklist to the participant
- The coach provides various LMI reports and website links that are related to the participant's journey

Activities
- Introduce LMI topic and review various LMI sources
- Browse each source and discuss how each could be helpful to inform career decisions
- Use the checklist to ensure one-by-one that the participant has an adequate understanding and that all remaining questions have been answered

Outcomes
- The participant has an awareness of the local LMI sources and has an understanding how to use the sources most relevant to their career planning

Labor Market Information (LMI) Checklist

There are numerous sources of labor market information. Sources may include federal data, state data, regional data, county data, city data, and employer specific information on jobs.

Check the boxes to indicate that your familiarity with these data sources:

- ☐ Federal Bureau of Labor Statistics (BLS)

- ☐ O*NET Median wages

- ☐ O*NET Employment

- ☐ O*NET Projected growth

- ☐ O*NET Projected job openings

- ☐ O*NET State trends

- ☐ State labor market data

- ☐ Local workforce board (WIB) data - Hot Jobs report

- ☐ Regional talent reports with supply-demand data

- ☐ Regional economic development organizations

- ☐ Employer specific job openings and trends

Tool 15 - Step 1.4
ETS Targets for Cognitive Assessment

Purpose

- The ETS Development Targets for Cognitive Ability provide information on the score levels of Prose, Document, and Quantitative skills that are generally associated with good job performance in each of the job families.
- Participants have a guide so they can determine if their cognitive skills are aligned with the jobs being considered and if they need to include foundational skill building in their development plan.

Inputs

- The coach provides the participant with the ETS Development Targets for Cognitive Ability

Activities

- The coach provides an introduction and overview
- The coach probes for understanding and answers the participant's questions

Outcomes

- The participant has an awareness of varying cognitive skill demands for various jobs
- The participant has a tool to understand cognitive skill requirements for jobs options they will evaluate

GoodPaths - ETS Cognitive Score Targets for Prose (P), Document (D), and Quantitative (Q)		P	D	Q	Total
Zone 1					
1	Food Preparation Zn1 — Cooks, Food Preparation Workers, Meat and Fish Trimers	2	3	2	7
2	Food Service Zn1 — Cafeteria, Concession, Coffee Shop, Baristas, Waiters, Waiters, Hosts	2	3	2	7
3	Clerk Zn1 — Cashiers, Counter and Rental Clerks	3	3	3	9
4	Washers Cleaners — Laundry, Dry-Cleaning, Pressers, Textile, Garment, Dishwashers	2	2	2	6
Zone 2					
5	Clerk Zn2 — Customer Service, Billing, Marking, Office, Order, Payroll, Shipping, Stock	3	3	3	9
6	Drivers — Drivers, Industrial Truck Operators, Delivery Services	2	3	3	8
7	Environmental Services — Cleaners of Vehicles, Janitors and Cleaners, Maids and Housekeepers	3	3	2	8
8	Food Preparation Zn2 — Bakers, Butchers, Cooks, Roasting, Drying, Batchmakers, Bartenders	3	3	3	9
9	Maintenance Repair Zn2 — Auto, Watercraft, Bicycle, Outdoor Power Equipment, Tire, and Shoe	3	3	3	9
10	Operators — Office Machines, Photographic Machines, Switchboard, and Telephone	3	3	2	8
11	Production — Recycling, Reclamation, Collectors, Inspectors, Testers, Sorters, Packers	3	3	2	8
12	Sales — Demonstrate, Promote, Parts, Pharmacy	3	3	3	9
13	Security — Security Guards and Retail Loss Prevention Specialists	3	3	2	8
14	Stock Logistics — Freight Stock, Material Movers, Order Fillers	2	3	2	7
15	Supervisors Zn2 — Food, Helpers, Labor, Material Movers, Housekeeping, Production, Sales	3	3	3	9
Zone 3					
16	Clerks Zn3 — Bookkeeping, Procurement, Production Planning, Executive Assistants	3	3	3	9
17	Food Preparation Zn3 — Chefs, Head Cooks, Private Cooks	3	3	3	9
18	Maintenance Repair Zn3 — Computer, Office Machine, Electronics, Automotive, Motorcycle, Appliance	3	3	3	9
19	Managers Zn3 — Administrative Services, Food Services	3	4	3	10
20	Professionals Zn3 — Buyers, Credit, Sales, Human Resources	3	3	3	9
21	Supervisors Zn3 — Office and Administrative, Mechanics, Installers, Repairers	3	3	3	9
22	Technicians — Computer, Quality, Display, Audio Video, Pharmacy, Optician, Electronic, Tailors, Jewelers	3	3	3	9
Zone 4					
23	Managers Zn4 — Advertising, Compensation, Computers, Marketing, Purchasing, Supply Chain	3	4	3	10
24	Professionals Zn4 — Accountants, Buyers, Compensation, Fraud, Information, Logistics, Marketing, Software, Development	3	4	3	10
Zone 5					
25	Executives — Chief Executives	4	4	4	12
26	Professionals Zn5 — Audiologists, Economists, Management Analysts, Dietitians, Nutritionists, Optometrists, Pharmacists	3	4	3	10

Tool 16 - Step 1.5
ETS Career Development Guides for Assessment

Purpose
- The ETS Targets for Career Development provide information on the score ranges for each behavioral competency that are generally associated with good job performance in each of the job families.
- Participants have a guide so they can determine if their behavioral skills are aligned with the jobs being considered and if they need to include foundational skill building in their development plan.

Inputs
- The coach provides the participant with the ETS Career Development Guides that include target ranges

Activities
- The coach provides an introduction and overview
- The coach probes for understanding and answers the participant's questions

Outcomes
- The participant has an awareness of varying behavioral skill demands for various jobs
- The participant has a tool to understand behavioral skill requirements for jobs options they will evaluate

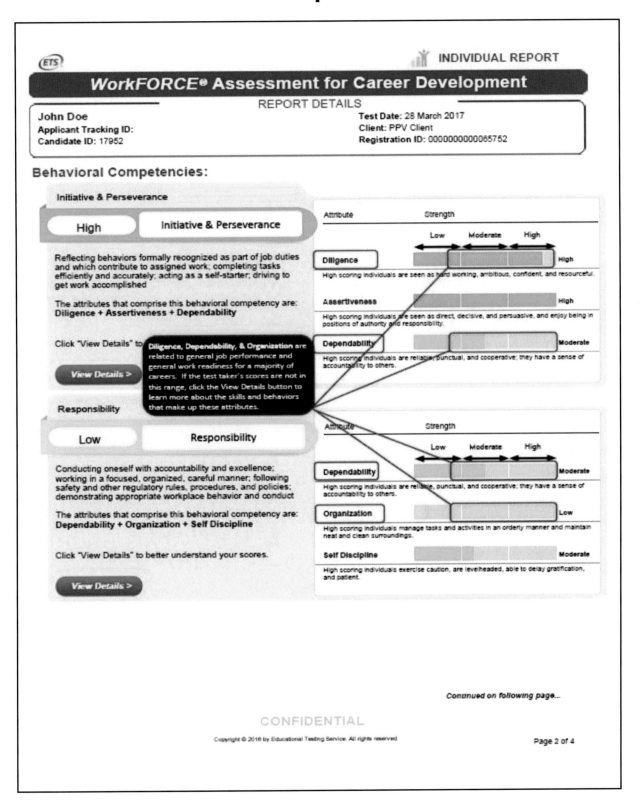

Tool 17 - Step 1.6
Interpretation Guide for O*NET Profiler

Purpose
- Interpretation guidance is an important function to enable the participant to gain the most insight from the O*NET Interest Profiler.

Inputs
- The O*NET Interest Profiler includes interpretation support within the online tool
- The RIASEC interest profile is illustrated and links to learn more are provided in the report
- The RIASEC profile is compared to O*NET data to provide the participant with a list of occupational titles that match the interest profile

Activities
- After answering the 60 questions in the online O*NET Interest Profiler:
  - Participant reflects upon RIASEC profile
  - Participant reflects upon the list of occupational titles to inform the initial steps in occupation exploration

Outcomes
- Participant has a short list of occupational titles that match their RIASEC profile

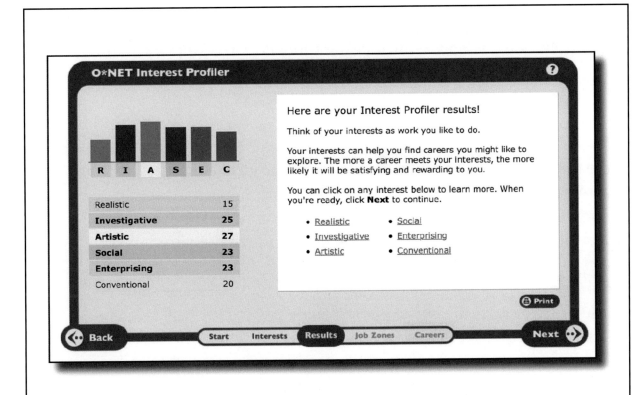

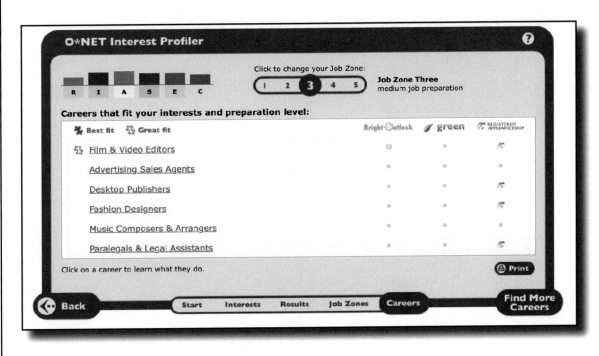

Tool 18 - Step 1.7
Interpretation Guide for ETS DEV

Purpose
- Interpretation guidance is an important function to enable the participant to gain the most insight from the ETS Development assessment.

Inputs
- The interpretation guide is a resource that is available to the coach so they are fully competent to guide the participant to accurately interpret their assessment results
- The ETS Cognitive assessment includes definitions on the score reports and interpretation guidance in the career development guides

Activities
- The coach reviews the interpretation guide prior to the Self-Awareness session to ensure a clear and accurate interpretation of the assessment results

Outcomes
- Coach has a comprehensive understanding of the assessment contents and proper interpretation
- Participant is guided by the coach to accurately interpret their assessment scores

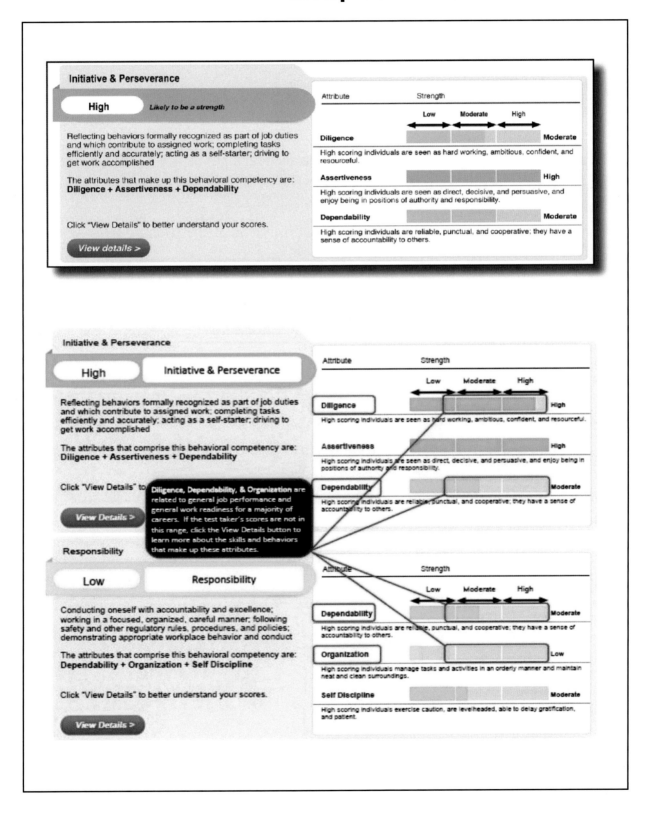

Tool 19 - Step 1.8
Interpretation Guide for ETS Cognitive

Purpose
- Interpretation guidance is an important function to enable the participant to gain the most insight from the ETS Cognitive assessment.

Inputs
- The interpretation guide is a resource that is available to the coach so they are fully competent to guide the participant to accurately interpret their assessment results
- The ETS Cognitive assessment includes definitions and interpretation guidance on the score reports

Activities
- The coach reviews the interpretation guide prior to the Self-Awareness session to ensure a clear and accurate interpretation of the assessment results

Outcomes
- Coach has a comprehensive understanding of the assessment contents and proper interpretation
- Participant is guided by the coach to accurately interpret their assessment scores

Individual Profile

WorkFORCE® Assessment for Cognitive Ability

READING PROSE DETAILED REPORT

Candidate Name: Jane Doe
Applicant Tracking ID: 1234-5678
Candidate ID: 1234-5678

Date Test Started: 9/15/16
Date Test Completed: 9/15/16
Client: XYZ Corporation

Reading Prose Score: **310 LEVEL 3**

Your Reading Prose score is in the **Level 3** range on Workforce for Cognitive Ability. At this level, you have the skills to cope with most demands of everyday life. You might sometimes find it challenging to use your skills with very unfamiliar, long or complex texts.

What is Reading Prose Skill?

Reading Prose skill involves understanding and using information found in materials such as newspaper articles, brochures, magazine articles, novels, manuals or flyers. All of these materials are examples of prose texts. Texts is a word for printed or written materials of all types.

You are using Reading Prose skills when you:

- Learn ways to quit smoking from a brochure at your health clinic
- Read a story or poem to a child
- Follow instructions in an owner's manual for assembling a product

Skills and Recommendations:

Current Skills

In general, you can usually do things like:

- Understanding and using a variety of reading materials, including newspaper and magazine articles, textbooks, manuals, brochures and flyers.
- Making inferences based on information in reading material by figuring out information that is not clearly and directly stated — in other words, "reading between the lines."
- Interpreting what you read and finding supporting examples.
- Locating information that is found in a few different sentences or paragraphs rather than in a single sentence — for example, finding three fire safety hazards explained in several different paragraphs of a home safety brochure.

Sample task you would be likely to successfully complete:

- Explaining two safety features a bicycle helmet should have using an article in which that information is not labeled as "safety features."

Skills to Strengthen

- Understanding and using long and complicated printed materials.
- Comparing and contrasting information in longer reading materials.
- Being able to summarize information you read.

Skills to Build in the Future

- Using prose texts to answer questions with multiple conditions — for example, finding a job listed in the want ads that meets three conditions: flexible hours, good hourly wage and location close to home.
- Interpreting information and ideas contained in various types of reading materials.
- Using background knowledge of different topics to facilitate and enhance your understanding of what you read.
- Being able to integrate information you read.

Tool 20 - Step 1.9
Probing Questions Assessments Debrief

Purpose
- The probing questions for assessments provide the coach with a menu of questions that can be used to probe the participant's interpretation and understanding of their assessment results.

Inputs
- The list of probing questions is a resource that is available to the coach so they are fully prepared to discuss assessment results with the participant

Activities
- The coach uses appropriate probing questions for each of the three assessments to guide a deeper discussion of assessment results
- The coach dialogs with the participant to discuss the holistic picture of the participant's skills, strengths, and weaknesses based on the three assessments, using further probing questions as needed

Outcomes
- Participant has a comprehensive, holistic, and accurate views of self based on assessments

Tool 20 - Step 1.9
Probing Questions Assessments Debrief

Probing Questions for Assessments

The following questions can be used to probe participants understanding and interpretation of their assessment results.

Questions to probe the O*NET Interest Profiler results:

☐ What is your RAISEC Profile?

☐ Are your top three interests in the order you expected?

☐ Which jobs are a good fit for your profile?

☐ Which ones seem like good recommendations?

☐ Which ones seem odd?

☐ Why?

Questions to probe the ETS Cognitive assessment results:

☐ What are your PDQ scores?

☐ What are the definitions of these three skills?

☐ Do these scores reflect your skills?

☐ Which one, if any, is surprising?

☐ Why?

Questions to probe the ETS Development assessment results:

☐ What are your six behavioral competency scores?

☐ What are the definitions of these six skills?

☐ Do these scores reflect your skills?

☐ Which one, if any, is surprising?

☐ Why?

Tool 21 - Step 1.10
Resume Checklist

Purpose
- The resume checklist provides an objective means to evaluate the quality of a resume and identify opportunities for improvement.

Inputs
- The resume checklist is a resource available to support resume reviews

Activities
- The coach will use the resume checklist to review the resume and provide suggestions for improvement during coaching sessions
- The coach and participant discuss the suggestions for improvement and agree upon items for the participant to address in the next version of the resume

Outcomes
- Clarity regarding the characteristics of a quality resume
- Suggestions for resume improvement
- An improved resume

Resume' Checklist

First impression

- Does the resume look original and not based on a template?
- Is the resume inviting to read, with clear sections and ample white space?
- Does the design look professional rather than like a simple typing job?
- Is a career summary included so the reader immediately knows your value proposition?
- Is the resume's length and overall appearance appropriate given your career level and summary?

Appearance

- Does the resume provide a visually pleasing, polished presentation?
- Is the font appropriate for the career level and industry?
- Are there design elements (bullets, bolding, and lines) to guide readers' eyes through the document and highlight important content?
- Is there a good balance between text and white space?
- Are margins even on all sides?
- Are design elements like spacing and font size used consistently throughout the document?
- If the resume is longer than a page, does the second page contain a heading? Is the page break formatted correctly?

Resume sections

- Are all resume sections clearly labeled?
- Are sections placed in the best order to highlight your strongest credentials?
- Is your work history listed in reverse chronological order (most recent job first)?

Career goal

- Is the resume targeted to a specific career goal, as opposed to a one-size-fits-all document?
- If this is a resume for a career change, does it include supporting details that show how your past experience is relevant to the new job?

Accomplishments

- Does the resume include a solid listing of your career accomplishments?
- Are accomplishments quantified by using numbers, percentages, dollar amounts, or other concrete measures of success?
- Do accomplishment statements begin with strong, varied action verbs?
- Are your accomplishments separated from your responsibilities?

Relevance

- Is the information relevant to hiring managers' needs?
- Does your resume's content support your career summary?
- Did you include keywords, appropriate buzzwords, and industry acronyms?
- Is applicable, additional information (awards and affiliations) included, and is personal information unrelated to the job (marital status, age, nationality) omitted?

Writing style

- Did you avoid writing the resume in an implied first-person voice with personal pronouns (I, me, and my)?
- Is the content flow logical and easy to understand?
- Is the resume as perfect as possible, with no careless typos or spelling, grammar, or syntax errors?

Source: Moster.com

Tool 22 - Step 1.11
Top Jobs Worksheet

Purpose
- The Top Jobs worksheet provides an exercise for the participant to process the information from the O*NET Interest Profiler so they develop a short list of jobs that are good options to evaluate.

Inputs
- The Top Jobs worksheet is the first step to narrow down the list of opportunities from thousands of potential jobs to a short list of three to five jobs
- The coach introduces the worksheet and assigns the exercise as a homework assignment at the end of the Self-Awareness session

Activities
- The participant carefully considers the list of job titles identified by the O*NET Interest Profiler
- The participant selects the most attractive titles from the Interest Profiler to make a short list
- The participant uses the job family chart and the job titles chart to list local job titles for the selected jobs

Outcomes
- A short list of jobs to evaluate

Top Jobs Worksheet

Note your top three job choices below. Then record notes for each job for each item to compare the three top jobs.

O*NET Job Title:			
O*NET Job Code:			
Job Family:			
Local Job Title:			
RAISEC Profile:			
1 Tasks			
2 Skills			
3 Hours			
4 Compensation			

Tool 23 - Step 1.12
ETS Assessments Worksheet

Purpose
- The ETS Assessments worksheet provides an exercise for the participant to process the information from the ETS assessments to develop a related list of strengths and growth opportunities.
- The ETS Assessments worksheet is a step to translate assessment data into actionable data.

Inputs
- The coach introduces the worksheet and assigns the exercise as a homework assignment at the end of the Self-Awareness session

Activities
- The participant records the cognitive targets and development score ranges defined by the career development guides in the target job scores column
- The participant records the ETS assessment scores in the assessment scores column
- The participant compares the scores to the targets and places a checkmark in the appropriate column to identify each as a strength or growth opportunity

Outcomes
- A list of strengths and growth opportunities

ETS WorkFORCE Assessments Worksheet

ETS Cognitive: Enter the scores for your target job and the scores from your assessment, then place a check mark under strength or growth opportunity. ETS Development: Using the Job Aids for your target job; enter low, moderate, or high only for competencies and facets that are included in the ETS Job Aids. If your score is inside the target area, check strength, if outside check growth opportunity.

Composite Competencies & Facets	Target Job Scores	Assessment Scores	Strength	Growth Opportunity
Cognitive Skills:				
Prose				
Document				
Quantitative				
Initiative and Perseverance:				
Diligence				
Assertiveness				
Dependability				
Responsibility:				
Dependability				
Organization				
Self-Discipline				
Teamwork and Citizenship:				
Collaboration				
Generosity				
Customer Service Orientation:				
Collaboration				
Generosity				
Friendliness				
Problem Solving and Ingenuity:				
Creativity				
Intellectual Orientation				
Inquisitiveness				
Flexibility and Resilience:				
Stability				
Optimism				

Tool 24 - Step 2.1
Strengths Summary Worksheet

Purpose
- The strengths worksheet supports the participant to develop a holistic view of their strengths.

Inputs
- ETS assessments worksheet with cognitive and behavioral skill strengths
- JOFI skills worksheet with foundational skill strengths
- Transferable skills worksheet with occupational skill strengths

Activities
- Carefully review the strengths identified by the ETS assessments, JOFI skills, and transferable skills exercises
- Reflect upon the big picture of strengths and combine them into one list
- Record the most important strengths

Outcomes
- A holistic list of strengths

Tool 24 - Step 2.1
Strengths Summary Worksheet

Strengths Summary Worksheet

The purpose of this worksheet is to help you develop a holistic view of your strengths. Review and reflect upon your strengths as identified by the ETS cognitive assessment, the ETS development assessment, the JOFI skills exercise, and the transferrable skills exercise; and summarize them below.

#		
1		☐
2		☐
3		☐
4		☐
5		☐
6		☐
7		☐
8		☐

Tool 25 - Step 2.2
Growth Opportunities Worksheet

Purpose
- The growth opportunities worksheet supports the participant to develop a holistic view of their growth opportunities.

Inputs
- ETS assessments worksheet with cognitive and behavioral skill growth opportunities
- JOFI skills worksheet with foundational skill growth opportunities
- Transferable skills worksheet with occupational skill growth opportunities

Activities
- Carefully review the growth opportunities identified by the ETS assessments, JOFI skills, and transferable skills exercises
- Reflect upon the big picture of growth opportunities and combine them into one list
- Record the most important growth opportunities

Outcomes
- A holistic list of growth opportunities

Development Targets Summary Worksheet

The purpose of this worksheet is to help you develop a holistic view of your growth and development needs. Review and reflect upon your development opportunities as identified by the ETS cognitive assessment, the ETS development assessment, the JOFI skills exercise, and the transferrable skills exercise; and summarize them below.

#		
1		☐
2		☐
3		☐
4		☐
5		☐
6		☐
7		☐
8		☐

Tool 26 - Step 2.3
Option Exploration Questions

Purpose
- The probing questions provide the coach with a menu of questions that can be used to probe the participants thinking behind their choices for the jobs listed on the top jobs worksheet.

Inputs
- The list of probing questions is a resource that is available to the coach so they are fully prepared to discuss the top jobs list with the participant

Activities
- The coach uses appropriate probing questions for the top jobs worksheet to guide a deeper discussion of the participants career goals and aspirations
- The coach dialogs with the participant to discuss the thinking behind the list of top jobs

Outcomes
- The participant has a deeper understanding of their preferences, goals, and aspirations

Tool 26 - Step 2.3
Option Exploration Questions

	Option Exploration Questions:	Job:
	Option Exploration Questions	
	Review the following questions before beginning your exploration of jobs. As you explore, note some of your findings below. You may also want to find individuals that perform the job and ask questions to learn more.	
1	What are the main tasks for this job?	
2	What are the working hours for this job?	
3	Does it require special training, licenses, certificates, or degrees?	
4	What skills are required?	
5	What is the compensation range?	
6	What do people in the job like about it?	
7	What do people in the job dislike about it?	
8	Does this work fit your personality?	
9	Does this work contribte to the community?	
10	Does this work match my O*NET interests (RAISEC) profile?	

Tool 27 - Step 2.4
JOFI Skills Worksheet

Purpose
- The JOFI foundational skills worksheet provides an exercise for the participant to process foundational skills information from the O*NET to develop a list of strengths and growth opportunities.
- This is an exercise to support reflection upon and evaluation of foundational skills and to translate those insights into actionable data.

Inputs
- The coach introduces the worksheet and assigns the exercise as a homework assignment at the end of the Option Exploration session

Activities
- The participant records the JOFI skill levels for their target job in the target column
- The participant records the JOFI skill levels for their current and previous jobs in the next two columns
- The participant compares the scores to the target and places a checkmark in the appropriate column to identify each as a strength or growth opportunity

Outcomes
- A list of strengths and growth opportunities

Level	Goodpaths / Foundational Competencies	Regional Industry Sector: Retail / Job Family: Clerks Zone-2	Target	Current	Previous	Strength	Opport.
		Navigation Exercise					
		Cognitive Communication Competencies					
4	Listening	Listening to others to receive verbal information.	50				
4	Speaking	Speaking to others to convey verbal information.	48				
4	Reading	Reading documents, charts, graphs, tables, forms, prose, and continuous texts.	48				
4	Writing	Writing to convey or document written information.	42				
		Cognitive Reasoning Competencies					
4	Reasoning	Logical thinking that influences the use of information in problem solving.	42				
4	Math	Quantitative thinking and use of mathematical methods.	46				
4	Information Skills	Obtaining, processing, analyzing, and documenting information.	57				
3	Judgment & Decision Making	Critical thinking, problem solving, judgment and decision making.	39				
		Character Competencies					
VI	Achievement Orientation	Personal goal setting, trying to succeed at those goals, and striving to be competent in own work.	66				
VI	Social Influence - Leadership	Having an impact on others in the organization and displaying energy and leadership.	56				
VI	Interpersonal Orientation	Being pleasant, cooperative, sensitive to others, easy to get a long with, and having a preference for associating with other organizational members.	85				
VI	Adjustment	Maturity, poise, flexibility, and restraint to cope with pressure, stress, criticism, setbacks, personal and work-related problems.	74				
VI	Conscientiousness	Dependability, commitment to doing the job correctly and carefully, and being trustworthy, accountable, and attentive to details.	88				
VI	Independence	Developing one's own ways of doing things, guiding oneself with little or no supervision, and depending on oneself to get things done.	75				
VI	Practical Intelligence	Generating useful ideas and thinking things through logically.	59				
		Physical Competencies					
3	Fine Manipulation	Related to the manipulation of objects.	26				
2	Control Movements	Related to the control and manipulation of objects in time and space.	10				
1	Reaction & Speed	Related to the speed of manipulation of objects.	NA	NA	NA		
1	Strength	Related to the capacity to exert force.	NA	NA	NA		
1	Endurance	Related to physical exertion over long periods of time.	NA	NA	NA		
1	Flexibility Balance & Coordination	Related to control of gross body movements.	NA	NA	NA		
4	Vision	Related to visual sensory input.	43				

Tool 28 - Step 2.5
Transferable Skills Worksheet

Purpose
- The transferable skills worksheet provides an exercise for the participant to process occupational skills information from the O*NET to develop a list of strengths and growth opportunities.
- This is an exercise to support reflection upon and evaluation of occupational skills and to translate those insights into actionable data.

Inputs
- The coach introduces the worksheet and assigns the exercise as homework at the end of the Option Exploration session

Activities
- The participant records the skill levels for their target job in the target column
- The participant records the skill levels for their current and previous jobs in the next two columns
- The participant compares the scores to the target and places a checkmark in the appropriate column to identify each as a strength or growth opportunity

Outcomes
- A list of strengths and growth opportunities

Tool 28 - Step 2.5
Transferable Skills Worksheet

Transferable Skills Worksheet

The transferable skills worksheet is designed to help you understand the skills that you have gained from previous jobs. These are skills that you will bring with you to your next job. The O*NET provides information on 41 Generalized Work Activities (GWAs). The 41 GWAs are work activities that are common across all jobs. Not all 41 are important to each job. If some GWAs are not important for your target job, the worksheet will have NA (Not Applicable) by those items. For each of the important GWAs the worksheet has level scores for your previous job, your current job, and your target job. Your work is to compare the scores in those three columns for each of the GWAs. If the scores in the first two columns are equal to or higher than the target job put a check mark in the strength column. If the scores are lower put a check mark in the opportunity column.

GWA	Transferable Skills (Generalized Work Activities)	Previous Job	Current Job	Target Job	Strength	Opportunity
1	Getting Information					
2	Monitor Processes, Materials, or Surroundings					
3	Identifying Objects, Actions, and Events					
4	Inspecting Equipment, Structures, or Material					
5	Estimating the Quantifiable Characteristics of Products, Events, or Information					
6	Judging the Qualities of Things, Services, or People					
7	Processing Information					
8	Evaluating Information to Determine Compliance with Standards					
9	Analyzing Data or Information					
10	Making Decisions and Solving Problems					
11	Thinking Creatively					
12	Updating and Using Relevant Knowledge					
13	Developing Objectives and Strategies					
14	Scheduling Work and Activities					
15	Organizing, Planning, and Prioritizing Work					
16	Performing General Physical Activities					
17	Handling and Moving Objects					
18	Controlling Machines and Processes					
19	Operating Vehicles, Mechanized Devices, or Equipment					
20	Interacting With Computers					
21	Drafting, Laying Out, and Specifying Technical Devices, Parts, and Equipment					
22	Repairing and Maintaining Mechanical Equipment					
23	Repairing and Maintaining Electronic Equipment					
24	Documenting/Recording Information					
25	Interpreting the Meaning of Information for Others					
26	Communicating with Supervisors, Peers, or Subordinates					
27	Communicating with Persons Outside Organization					
28	Establishing and Maintaining Interpersonal Relationships					
29	Assisting and Caring for Others					
30	Selling or Influencing Others					
31	Resolving Conflicts and Negotiating with Others					
32	Performing for or Working Directly with the Public					
33	Coordinating the Work and Activities of Others					
34	Developing and Building Teams					
35	Training and Teaching Others					
36	Guiding, Directing, and Motivating Subordinates					
37	Coaching and Developing Others					
38	Provide Consultation and Advice to Others					
39	Performing Administrative Activities					
40	Staffing Organizational Units					
41	Monitoring and Controlling Resources					

Tool 29 - Step 2.6
ESM Worksheet

Purpose
- The ESM worksheet provides an opportunity to pause and evaluate the big picture in terms of three major options: (1) pursue an educational and training path, (2) pursue a job search path, or (3) recognize that the current job is a great fit and pursue a mastery path.
- Sometimes the current job is optimal. Sometimes formal education and training is not the right next step. It is good to pause and reflect upon the implications of these options.

Inputs
- The coach introduces the worksheet and assigns the exercise as homework at the end of the Option Exploration session

Activities
- The participant takes time to reflect on the big picture by comparing the ESM options
- The participant records their decision on the worksheet

Outcomes
- A confirmation or adjustment of the path forward

ESM Worksheet

The purpose of this worksheet is to ensure thoughtful consideration of the three major options for career advancement:

1. Education and Training Option - Your best next step is to seek out formal education and training, enroll in a program, and earn another degree or credential.

2. Job Search Option - You are currently "job ready" for another position and should move forward with job search activities.

3. Mastery Option - After some career exploration and reflection, you realize that your current job is the best job for you. Rather than changing jobs, you are best served by focusing your energy on achieving mastery in your current job.

After reflection on the above three choices my decision is to pursue:

☐ Education and Training Option

☐ Job Search Option

☐ Mastery Option

Tool 30 - Step 3.1
Career Pathways Discussion Checklist

Purpose

- The purpose of the career pathways discussion checklist is to review the essential elements from an individual perspective.

Inputs

- The checklist is a resource available to the coach to prepare for a discussion of career pathways with the participant that occurs in the Decision Making step

Activities

- Review the checklist
- Provide an introduction and overview of the checklist to the participant
- Dialog and answer questions on career pathways

Outcomes

- The participant has a clear understanding of career pathways and how that concept can be helpful to them

Career Pathways Discussion Checklist

The purpose of this worksheet is to review the essential elements of career pathways from an individuals perspective.

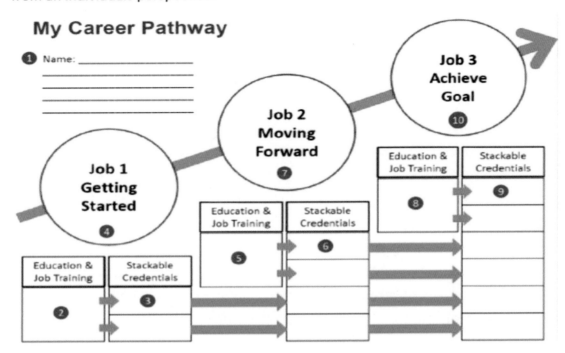

The concept of career pathways is presented differently in different settings. In the K-12 setting, career pathways are generally presented as broad pathways that lead to jobs in broad categories such as: retail, health care, or manufacturing. In the postsecondary setting, career pathways are generally presented as pathways to a degree that will open doors to certain types of jobs. In the workforce setting, career pathways are generally about moving from one job to the next, and the next. All of these perspectives are correct. You are likely to encounter each of them as you read and speak about career pathways.

A great career is a series of great jobs ... jobs that are right for you.

Many people have 10 to 20 different jobs over a lifetime. It is helpful to have a plan for your progression through the next two or three jobs. A clear view of the next two or three jobs will help inform better decision making.

Tool 31 - Step 3.2
Career Pathway MAP (My Action Plan)

Purpose
- The career pathways action plan provides a guide to illustrate the participants career plans including job progression; education, training, and credentialing; and support needed.

Inputs
- The career pathways action plan is introduced in the Decision Making step

Activities
- An introduction and overview is provided by the coach
- Discussion around job progression, learning options, and support needed
- Draft notes from the discussion to prepare for the homework assignment
- The participant is assigned homework to complete the career pathways action plan

Outcomes
- A personalized career pathway that illustrates job progression; education, training, and credentialing; and support needed

Tool 31 - Step 3.2
Career Pathway MAP (My Action Plan)

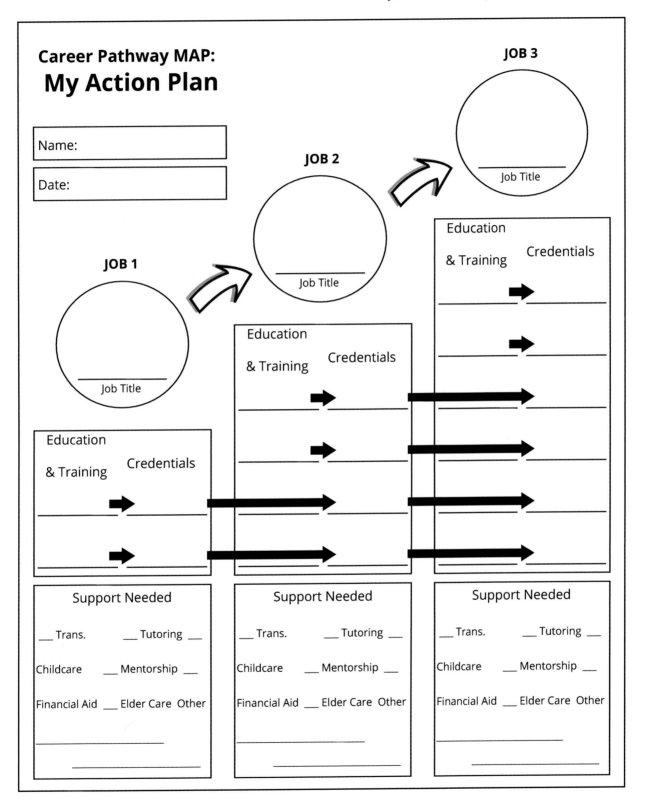

Tool 32 - Step 3.3
Decision Making Checklist

Purpose
- The decision making checklist provides an opportunity to confirm that the participant's career path is in alignment with each of the information sources developed throughout the coaching process.

Inputs
- The decision making checklist is assigned as homework at the end of the Decision Making step

Activities
- After the participant drafts the career pathway action plan they review the checklist to confirm that the pathway is in alignment with each item

Outcomes
- Confirmation and assurance that the participant's career pathway is optimal based on multiple sources of information

Decision Making Checklist

It is best to consider a broad set of relevant information when making decisions. The following sources of information should be considered to make an optimal career decision.

Check the boxes to indicate that your use of these data sources:

- ☐ Cognitive assessments scores relative to targets

- ☐ Behavioral assessments scores (ETS DEV) relative to targets

- ☐ JOFI Foundational Skills

- ☐ Transferrable Skills

- ☐ Strengths from the strengths summary

- ☐ Development opportunities

- ☐ Labor market information (LMI)

- ☐ Access to programs at various schools

- ☐ Transportation and travel time to attend various programs

- ☐ Financial means and support

- ☐ Family support

After reflection on the above information my conclusion is to confirm or change my target job decision:

- ☐ Confirm

- ☐ Change

Tool 33 - Step 3.4
Learning Options Worksheet

Purpose
- The learning options worksheet provides an exercise to help the participant evaluate options to acquire the skills needed for job progression.

Inputs
- The learning options worksheet is assigned as homework at the end of the Decision Making session

Activities
- Review the growth opportunities worksheet
- List formal education and training options that would address selected growth opportunities
- List work-based learning options that would address selected growth opportunities

Outcomes
- A list of formal education and training options and work-based learning options to grow the skills needed for job progression

Learning Options Worksheet

Take a few moments to reflect on your growth and development targets. Think about which skills require formal education and training and which skills can be learned at work. Then search for education and training options that will enable you to achieve your learning objectives. Record those here:

	Institution	Program
Education and Training Options		

Then think about assignments at work that would enable you to learn new skills related to your growth and development targets. And think about the managers that will need to approve those assignments. Record those here:

	Potential work assignments	Supporting Manager
Work-Based Learning Options		

Tool 34 - Step 4.1
To Do List of Next Actions

Purpose
- The next actions worksheet provides a means for the participant to move from planning to action.

Inputs
- The worksheet is introduced and discussed during the Action Planning step

Activities
- Next actions (To Do List) are discussed
- Notes are recorded by the participant during dialog with the coach
- The next actions are recorded on the list as homework
- Next actions guide the activities of the Follow-Up step
- The next actions are updated as progress is made in the Follow-Up step

Outcomes
- Actions are accomplished to move the participant forward
- Ultimately the participant secures a position in their target job

Tool 34 - Step 4.1
To Do List of Next Actions

To Do List - Next Actions Worksheet

The purpose of this worksheet is to help you organize a set of next actions based on your Career Path MAP (My Action Plan) and summarize them below. Use the column on the right to set target dates for each of your next actions.

1		
2		
3		
4		
5		
6		
7		
8		

Chapter 6 | Career Coaching Technology (Assessments)

The career coaching process described in chapter four is supported by the tools described in chapter five. The ease-of-use of the tools can be improved by leveraging technology. At this stage, the coaching process recommended above leverages the O*NET website and ETS WorkFORCE Assessments. This chapter introduces those essential technology solutions.

Assessments are a key part of the evidence-based career coaching process. They are the basis of the critical first step in which participants develop the self-awareness that will allow them to narrow their possible job paths and guide any training and education plans they wish to make.

These assessments will be of three kinds:

1. Career Interests Assessments
2. Cognitive Assessments
3. Personality Assessments

After a brief description of each kind of test, we have provided an additional description of a specific test that we have used in our work. See the Appendices for additional materials, including full examples of score reports.

1. Career Interests Assessments

Career Interests Assessments help a person find out what their interests are and how they relate to the world of work. With this information a person can make a better decision about the kind of career they wish to pursue. Kuder is a well known leader in this space, while Naviance and Career Cruising also offer a large

variety of products. A free and very basic assessment is available through O*NET online, which we describe throughout this chapter. The O*NET Interest Profiler can be found at mynextmove.org (see the "Tell us what you like to do" link).

The O*NET Interest Profiler

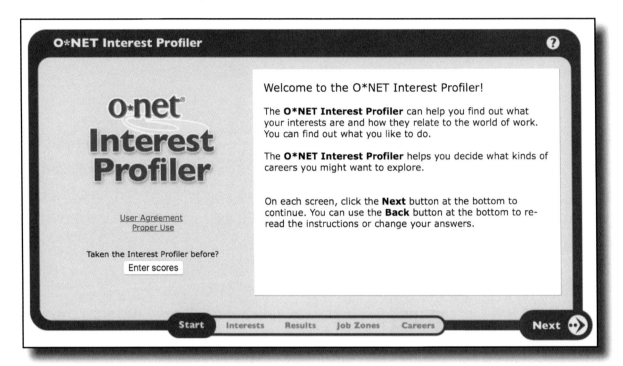

Figure 6.1: O*NET Interest Profiler Homepage

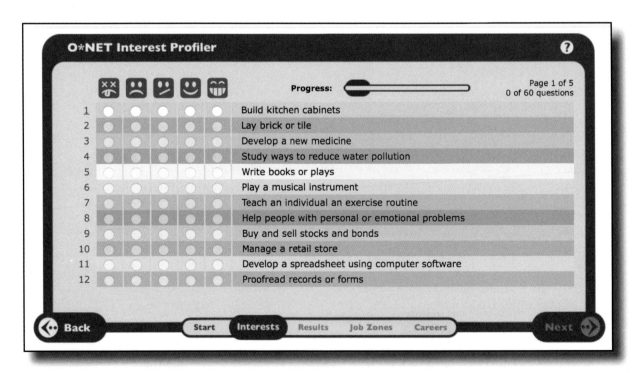

Figure 6.2: Example of O*NET Interest Profiler Questions

The assessment asks 60 questions about work activities characteristic of various kinds of work, and asks the test taker to rate how he or she feels about those activities on a five-point scale from Strongly Dislike to Strongly Like. The survey also asks individuals not to worry about whether they currently have enough education or about how much money they would make.

The scores are provided for the following categories: Realistic, Investigative, Artistic, Social, Enterprising, and Conventional (RIASEC Model). Based on the scores, individuals can clink links that show more detail about the interests that define the work they like to do.

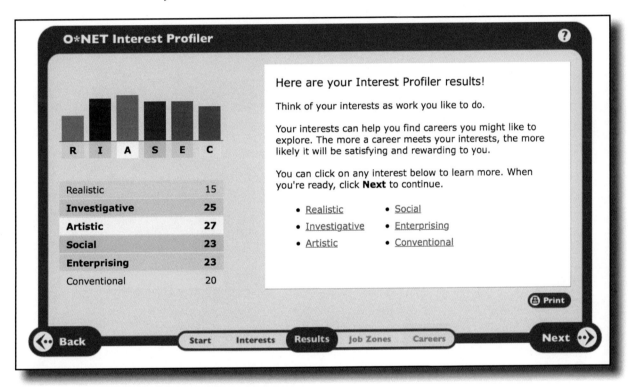

*Figure 6.3: Example of O*NET Interest Profiler Results*

The next section of the assessment asks how much preparation the participant will need or is willing to undertake and divides occupations into five zones requiring various levels of credentials and education. These zones are explained in links. Once the participant makes that decision, the O*NET Interests Profiler generates a list of potential occupations that participants can explore.

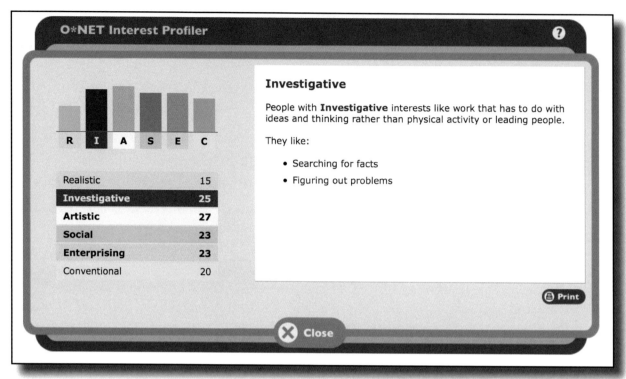

Figure 6.4: Example of O*NET Interest Profiler "Investigative" Interests

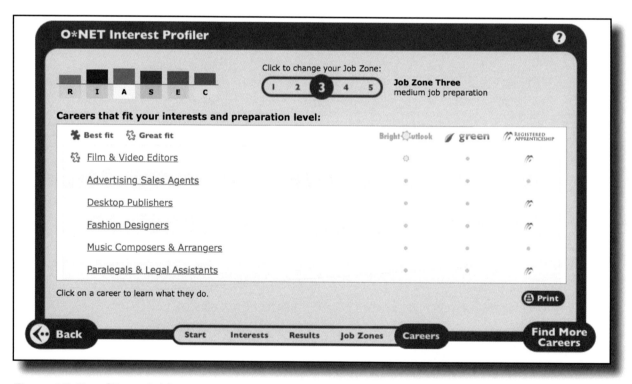

Figure 6.5: List of Potential Occupations

As mentioned in Chapter 4, career coaches should use career interests assessments to guide participants during the "Self-Awareness" step. Comparing career and training interests to a regional "hot jobs" list and growth projections in O*NET should yield a short list of jobs that participants can research as homework. Part of the investigation can compare the participant's strengths and skill and training challenges with job expectations and requirements so that informed decision making is tied to current realities and future goals.

Career coaches might probe career interests by asking questions such as these:

- How do you feel about the results of the assessment? Do these interests seem right?
- What do you think about your most and least similar occupations based on interest fit? Which did you find to most engage your interests?
- Compare your regions "hot jobs" list. Any matches?
- What about your career intentionality? [Note to what degree the participant communicates positive intent, confidence, and benefit around the training and job search.]
- Showing the participant how to use career interests to search the O*NET, probe in the Option Exploration about a few of the jobs the candidate finds: are you ready to take that job? Do you think you need additional education and training first?

2. Cognitive Assessments

Cognitive assessments measure cognitive abilities such as various kinds of reading skills, math or quantitative ability, and sometimes even attention, perception or motor skills. There are many companies that offer cognitive testing products designed for high stakes testing. ACT WorkKeys and ETS WorkFORCE assessments are examples of cognitive assessments. Following is a brief introduction to some of these ETS products.

ETS WorkFORCE Assessment for Cognitive Ability measures basic cognitive skills including Reading Prose, Reading Documents, and Quantitative Abilities. The 60-90 minute, web-based assessment consists of a short set of background questions, plus three sets of reading prose, reading documents and quantitative real-world tasks. It is designed to measure the abilities needed for a particular

position employers are seeking to fill, and can be used in the hiring process in various industries when considering new employees for targeted positions or within training programs designed to help prepare individuals for targeted positions. From the standpoint of career coaching, this assessment can also be used to measure an individual's current proficiency or progress in the skills over time.

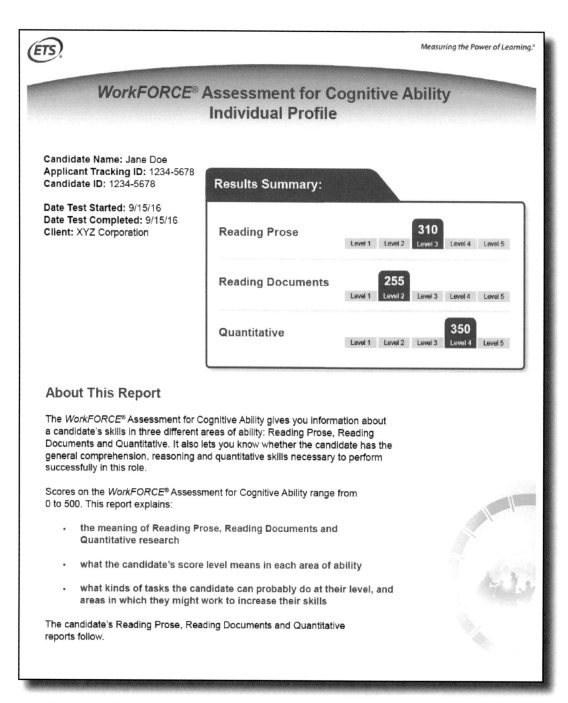

Figure 6.6: ETS WorkFORCE Assessment for Cognitive Ability Results Summary

Scores for each area (ranging from 0-500) are explained in separate sections. For example:

Reading Prose (how well individuals understand and use information found in newspapers, magazines, novels, manuals or other text in paragraph form).

Figure 6.7: Reading Prose Score Example

Reading Documents (the knowledge and skills required by an individual to locate and use information contained in job applications or payroll forms, bus schedules, maps, indexes and several types of information).

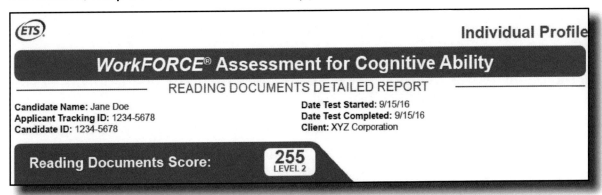

Figure 6.8: Reading Documents Score Example

Quantitative Abilities (the knowledge and skills required by an individual to apply arithmetic operations embedded in printed materials, as in balancing a checkbook, figuring out a tip, completing an order form or determining the amount of interest on a loan).

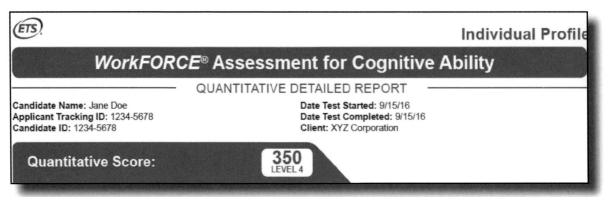

Figure 6.9: Quantitative Score Example

3. Personality Assessments

Personality assessments measure an individual's behavioral or character traits. There are many well-known forms of personality assessments, such as the Myers Briggs Type Indicator or the Minnesota Multiphasic Personality Inventory. An important distinction is whether the test in question is suitable for selection and hiring. Tests by ETS, Hogan and others have been shown to be measurably related to job performance. Aligning to these assessments will be most beneficial for career coaching.

For example, the ETS WorkFORCE Program for Career Development is designed to help support employee and prospective employee success by identifying the behavioral skills most needed to train and develop for an individual's role or intended role. The assessment consists of (1) a behavioral assessment, which is the WorkFORCE Assessment for Career Development and (2) a behavioral training program—the WorkFORCE Training Program for Career Development—that parallels the competencies measured in the assessment.

The WorkFORCE Assessment for Career Development measures 6 key behavioral competencies & 13 underlying behavioral attributes proven to be associated with likelihood of workplace success. The 20-minute assessment generates an Individual Profile for each prospective employee detailing his or her specific development strengths and needs in the following areas:

- Initiative & Perseverance: Being dedicated and willing to go the extra mile
- Problem Solving & Ingenuity: Being strong problem solvers

- Responsibility: Taking the job seriously
- Flexibility & Resilience: Having a positive and enthusiastic attitude
- Teamwork & Citizenship: Collaborating well with others
- Customer Service Orientation: Treating customers and peers with respect and consideration

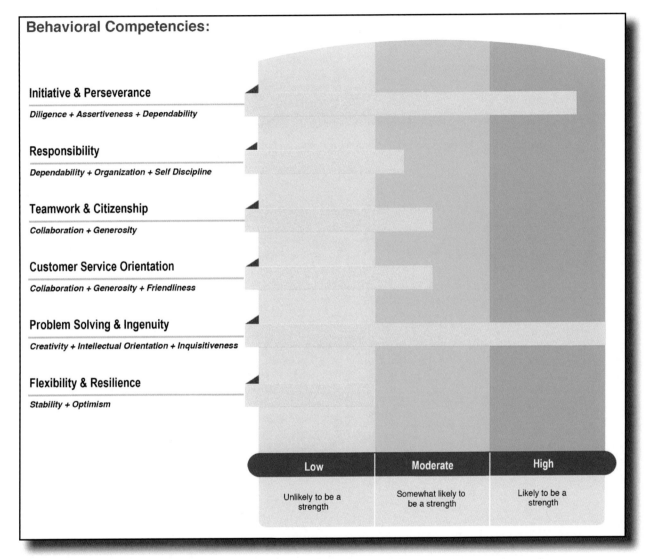

Figure 6.10: Example Summary Score Report for the WorkFORCE Assessment for Career Development

In the report, each Behavioral Competency is explained individually, and the competency is broken down into its personality facets. For example, Initiative & Perseverance is defined and broken down into Diligence, Assertiveness, and Dependability facets.

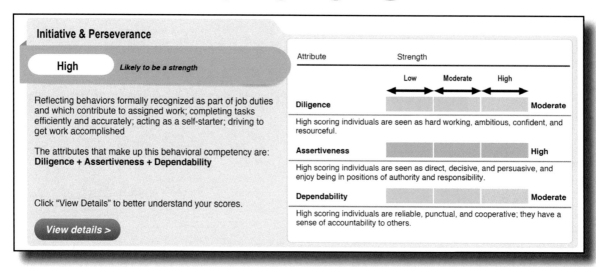

Initiative & Perseverance

High   *Likely to be a strength*

Reflecting behaviors formally recognized as part of job duties and which contribute to assigned work; completing tasks efficiently and accurately; acting as a self-starter; driving to get work accomplished

The attributes that make up this behavioral competency are:
Diligence + Assertiveness + Dependability

Click "View Details" to better understand your scores.

View details >

Attribute	Strength			
	Low	Moderate	High	
Diligence				Moderate
High scoring individuals are seen as hard working, ambitious, confident, and resourceful.				
Assertiveness				High
High scoring individuals are seen as direct, decisive, and persuasive, and enjoy being in positions of authority and responsibility.				
Dependability				Moderate
High scoring individuals are reliable, punctual, and cooperative; they have a sense of accountability to others.				

Figure 6.11: Detail of the Initiative and Perseverance Behavioral Competency

Section III

Education, Training, & Credentials

"Helping individuals understand the totality of their educational path is key. Empowering individuals as they build their skills and create stackable credentials will lead to long-term economic security."

the **comprehensive** approach

 CREDENTIALS: DEGREES AND LICENSES

 INDUSTRY-WIDE SKILLS AND CREDENTIALS

 OCCUPATIONAL SKILLS AND CREDENTIALS

 EMPLOYABILITY SKILLS AND CREDENTIALS

 FOUNDATIONAL SKILLS, MEASURES, AND CREDENTIALS

Chapter 7 | Foundational Skills, Measures, & Credentials

Foundational competencies refer to cognitive, character and physical skills and abilities. They are sometimes referred to as "soft skills" or "behavioral skills," although these names tend to refer to character skills more than cognitive or physical skills and abilities, which are equally important dimensions. Very few foundational skills credentials have achieved wide use within or across sectors. It is foundational competencies, however, that are often very good predictors of job performance. It is therefore important to identify which foundational competencies can be measurably linked to the occupational competencies for an occupation.

Establishing a link between foundation and occupational competencies requires an employer to undertake job analysis. To qualify as "evidence-based," foundational competencies should be determined by a job analysis process and confirmed by validation studies, not simply by discussion and consensus. Validation studies typically include logical linkages and analysis of quantitative data that establish the relationship between what a test actually measures and what it is intended to measure or predict. Employers validate the use of assessments by conducting validation studies that confirm competencies are job-related – that is, related to job performance ratings.

Contextualizing Foundational Skills

Education and training providers around the country have begun significant efforts to contextualize the delivery of foundational skills both inside and outside of the classroom. Contextualizing these skills refers to the process of linking foundational content to a specific discipline or training area. A basic example of this process would be the development of technical writing courses. Many post-secondary institutions currently have writing courses with a focus on business writing, artistic writing, or technical writing at the 100 level. Basic

foundational elements of writing remain as key learning objectives, but the content is focused on a discipline that is of greater interest to the student based on their defined career pathway and career aspirations.

There are significant and broad opportunities to further contextualize foundational skills content at both the secondary and post-secondary level, far beyond writing. Numerous proprietary vendors exist to do just this kind of work; further, some colleges and training providers have even developed their own curricula that is largely contextual. This is an effective approach for content delivery, especially for areas where students have traditionally struggled.

The topic of mathematics is important here, as we know, both anecdotally and through research. This area is consistently difficult for many individuals who need to achieve basic foundational competence as part of their career pathway. In the next section of this chapter we'll describe how we can peel away layers of broad content areas like math in order to more accurately and discreetly describe the basic math competencies that are needed for a specific job or job family. By doing this, we can also understand how to create curricula that is aligned with this more accurate and discreet description of math content that is needed. To say to an individual that math is a core competency needed for any number of jobs or job families is an overstatement; instead, we can say to a student here are the specific competencies, or learning objectives, within math that are needed, based on evidence, and here are the content areas that you will be taught. Developing contextualized curricula based on that prescription better serves the student and creates a more efficient classroom experience.

Talxcellenz® JOFI (Job Fit) Competencies

The US Department of Labor's online O*NET is the single greatest source for information about foundational and occupational competencies in each sector of the US economy. The raw data of the O*NET contains information on hundreds of elements, including 136 competency elements of knowledge, skills, abilities, and work styles (KSAs). In our work with subject matter experts (SMEs) during job analyses, we learned that this list was much too long to be useful. As a result, we grouped similar competencies into competency families so that SMEs could have coherent and productive conversations regarding the relative importance of various foundational competencies. Grouping competencies into

competency families allowed us to gather more accurate feedback from the SMEs. After a few iterations we defined a set of 22 competency families grouped into three sections: cognitive competencies, character competencies, and physical competencies. They are illustrated here:

Cognitive Communication Competencies		
Listening	**Listening to others to receive verbal information.**	
	Active Listening	Giving full attention to what other people are saying, taking time to understand the points being made, asking questions as appropriate, and not interrupting at inappropriate times.
	Oral Comprehension	The ability to listen to and understand information and ideas presented through spoken words and sentences.
	Speech Recognition	The ability to identify and understand the speech of another person.
Speaking	**Speaking to others to convey verbal information.**	
	Speaking	Talking to others to convey information effectively.
	Oral Expression	The ability to communicate information and ideas in speaking so others will understand.
	Speech Clarity	The ability to speak clearly so others can understand you.
Reading	**Reading documents, charts, graphs, tables, forms, prose, and continuous texts.**	
	Reading Comprehension	Understanding written sentences and paragraphs in work related documents.
	Written Comprehension	The ability to read and understand information and ideas presented in writing.
Writing	**Writing to convey or document written information.**	
	Writing	Communicating effectively in writing as appropriate for the needs of the audience.
	Written Expression	The ability to communicate information and ideas in writing so others will understand.

Cognitive Reasoning Competencies		
	Logical thinking that influences the use of information in problem solving.	
Reasoning	Problem Sensitivity	The ability to tell when something is wrong or is likely to go wrong. It does not involve solving the problem, only recognizing there is a problem.
	Deductive Reasoning	The ability to apply general rules to specific problems to produce answers that make sense.
	Inductive Reasoning	The ability to combine pieces of information to form general rules or conclusions (includes finding a relationship among seemingly unrelated events).
	Information Ordering	The ability to arrange things or actions in a certain order or pattern according to a specific rule or set of rules (e.g., patterns of numbers, letters, words, pictures, mathematical operations).
	Category Flexibility	The ability to generate or use different sets of rules for combining or grouping things in different ways.
	Quantitative thinking and use of mathematical methods.	
Math	Mathematics	Using mathematics to solve problems.
	Mathematical Reasoning	The ability to choose the right mathematical methods or formulas to solve a problem.
	Number Facility	The ability to add, subtract, multiply, or divide quickly and correctly.
	Obtaining, processing, analyzing, and documenting information.	
Information Skills	Getting Information	Observing, receiving, and otherwise obtaining information from all relevant sources.
	Processing Information	Compiling, coding, categorizing, calculating, tabulating, auditing, or verifying information or data.
	Analyzing Data or Information	Identifying the underlying principles, reasons, or facts of information by breaking down information or data into separate parts.
	Interacting With Computers	Using computers and computer systems (including hardware and software) to program, write software, set up functions, enter data, or process information.
	Documenting/Recording Information	Entering, transcribing, recording, storing, or maintaining information in written or electronic/magnetic form.

Judgment & Decision Making	**Critical thinking, problem solving, judgment and decision making.**	
	Critical Thinking	Using logic and reasoning to identify the strengths and weaknesses of alternative solutions, conclusions or approaches to problems.
	Active Learning	Understanding the implications of new information for both current and future problem-solving and decision-making.
	Complex Problem Solving	Identifying complex problems and reviewing related information to develop and evaluate options and implement solutions.
	Judgment and Decision Making	Considering the relative costs and benefits of potential actions to choose the most appropriate one.
	Updating and Using Relevant Knowledge	Keeping up-to-date technically and applying new knowledge to your job.

	Character Competencies	
Achievement Orientation	**Personal goal setting, trying to succeed at those goals, and striving to be competent in own work.**	
	Achievement/Effort	Job requires establishing and maintaining personally challenging achievement goals and exerting effort toward mastering tasks.
	Persistence	Job requires persistence in the face of obstacles.
	Initiative	Job requires a willingness to take on responsibilities and challenges.
Social Influence - Leadership	**Having an impact on others in the organization and displaying energy and leadership.**	
	Leadership	Job requires a willingness to lead, take charge, and offer opinions and direction.
	Monitoring	Monitoring/Assessing performance of yourself, other individuals, or organizations to make improvements or take corrective action.
	Coordination	Adjusting actions in relation to others' actions.
	Persuasion	Persuading others to change their minds or behavior.
	Negotiation	Bringing others together and trying to reconcile differences.
	Instructing	Teaching others how to do something.
	Time Management	Managing one's own time and the time of others.

Interpersonal Orientation	**Being pleasant, cooperative, sensitive to others, easy to get a long with, and having a preference for associating with other organizational members.**	
	Cooperation	Job requires being pleasant with others on the job and displaying a good-natured, cooperative attitude.
	Concern for Others	Job requires being sensitive to others' needs and feelings and being understanding and helpful on the job.
	Social Orientation	Job requires preferring to work with others rather than alone, and being personally connected with others on the job.
Adjustment	**Maturity, poise, flexibility, and restraint to cope with pressure, stress, criticism, setbacks, personal and work-related problems.**	
	Self Control	Job requires maintaining composure, keeping emotions in check, controlling anger, and avoiding aggressive behavior, even in very difficult situations.
	Stress Tolerance	Job requires accepting criticism and dealing calmly and effectively with high stress situations.
	Adaptability/Flexibility	Job requires being open to change (positive or negative) and to considerable variety in the workplace.
Conscientiousness	**Dependability, commitment to doing the job correctly and carefully, and being trustworthy, accountable, and attentive to details.**	
	Dependability	Job requires being reliable, responsible, and dependable, and fulfilling obligations.
	Attention to Detail	Job requires being careful about detail and thorough in completing work tasks.
	Integrity	Job requires being honest and ethical.
Independence	**Developing one's own ways of doing things, guiding oneself with little or no supervision, and depending on oneself to get things done.**	
	Independence	Job requires developing one's own ways of doing things, guiding oneself with little or no supervision, and depending on oneself to get things done.
	Independence	Occupations that satisfy this work value allow employees to work on their own and make decisions. Corresponding needs are Creativity, Responsibility and Autonomy.
Practical Intelligence	**Generating useful ideas and thinking things through logically.**	
	Innovation	Job requires creativity and alternative thinking to develop new ideas for and answers to work-related problems.
	Analytical Thinking	Job requires analyzing information and using logic to address work-related issues and problems.
	Investigative	Investigative occupations frequently involve working with ideas, and require an extensive amount of thinking. These occupations can involve searching for facts and figuring out problems mentally.

Physical Competencies		
	Related to the manipulation of objects.	
Fine Manipulation	Arm-Hand Steadiness	The ability to keep your hand and arm steady while moving your arm or while holding your arm and hand in one position.
	Manual Dexterity	The ability to quickly move your hand, your hand together with your arm, or your two hands to grasp, manipulate, or assemble objects.
	Finger Dexterity	The ability to make precisely coordinated movements of the fingers of one or both hands to grasp, manipulate, or assemble very small objects.
	Related to the control and manipulation of objects in time and space.	
Control Movements	Control Precision	The ability to quickly and repeatedly adjust the controls of a machine or a vehicle to exact positions.
	Multilimb Coordination	The ability to coordinate two or more limbs (for example, two arms, two legs, or one leg and one arm) while sitting, standing, or lying down. It does not involve performing the activities while the whole body is in motion.
	Response Orientation	The ability to choose quickly between two or more movements in response to two or more different signals (lights, sounds, pictures). It includes the speed with which the correct response is started with the hand, foot, or
	Rate Control	The ability to time your movements or the movement of a piece of equipment in anticipation of changes in the speed and/or direction of a moving object or scene.
	Related to the speed of manipulation of objects.	
Reaction & Speed	Reaction Time	The ability to quickly respond (with the hand, finger, or foot) to a signal (sound, light, picture) when it appears.
	Wrist-Finger Speed	The ability to make fast, simple, repeated movements of the fingers, hands, and wrists.
	Speed of Limb Movement	The ability to quickly move the arms and legs.
	Related to the capacity to exert force.	
Strength	Static Strength	The ability to exert maximum muscle force to lift, push, pull, or carry objects.
	Explosive Strength	The ability to use short bursts of muscle force to propel oneself (as in jumping or sprinting), or to throw an object.
	Dynamic Strength	The ability to exert muscle force repeatedly or continuously over time. This involves muscular endurance and resistance to muscle fatigue.
	Trunk Strength	The ability to use your abdominal and lower back muscles to support part of the body repeatedly or continuously over time without 'giving out' or fatiguing.

Endurance	**Related to physical exertion over long periods of time.**	
	Stamina	The ability to exert yourself physically over long periods of time without getting winded or out of breath.

Flexibility Balance & Coordination	**Related to control of gross body movements.**	
	Extent Flexibility	The ability to bend, stretch, twist, or reach with your body, arms, and/or legs.
	Dynamic Flexibility	The ability to quickly and repeatedly bend, stretch, twist, or reach out with your body, arms, and/or legs.
	Gross Body Coordination	The ability to coordinate the movement of your arms, legs, and torso together when the whole body is in motion.
	Gross Body Equilibrium	The ability to keep or regain your body balance or stay upright when in an unstable position.

Vision	**Related to visual sensory input.**	
	Near Vision	The ability to see details at close range (within a few feet of the observer).
	Far Vision	The ability to see details at a distance.
	Visual Color Discrimination	The ability to match or detect differences between colors, including shades of color and brightness.
	Night Vision	The ability to see under low light conditions.
	Peripheral Vision	The ability to see objects or movement of objects to one's side when the eyes are looking ahead.
	Depth Perception	The ability to judge which of several objects is closer or farther away from you, or to judge the distance between you and an object.
	Glare Sensitivity	The ability to see objects in the presence of glare or bright lighting.

Chapter 8

Employability Skills & Credentials

Employability Skills and Credentials, sometimes also referred to as work-readiness skills and certifications, are typically assessment-based credentials that have been designed to indicate to employers that individuals are ready to perform the basic tasks that an occupation requires. These credentials show that individuals possess the characteristics that have been identified as important to success in the workplace (usually corresponding to the foundational competencies discussed in the last chapter), as well as basic academic skills, such as math, reading, and computer skills. These competencies are intended to describe and measure behaviors that are common across industries and job families.

Employability skills and credentials have their roots in work done by the Secretary's Commission on Achieving Necessary Skills (SCANS) and the subsequent National Skills Standards Board (created by the 1994 National Skills Standards Act). Since then, work-readiness programs have proliferated, and credentials have multiplied. The following are some of the better-known examples:

- The National Career Readiness Certificate (NCRC), which is linked to ACT's WorkKeys program. The NCRC measures these skills and awards certification at different levels (platinum, gold, silver, or bronze) in order to indicate the types of jobs for which the candidate is qualified.
- The Comprehensive Adult Student Assessment Systems (CASAS) tests also measure basic academic skills, such as mathematics and reading, as well as some soft skills.
- The Skills USA Workplace Readiness Certificate Program, focuses primarily on abilities and personal qualities, such as problem solving, leadership, and ethics.

- ETS certificates include the ETS WorkFORCE Assessment for Cognitive Ability, ETS WorkFORCE Assessment for Career Development, and ETS WorkFORCE Career Foundations Certificate.
- Some states and localities have developed their own, local, credentialing and assessment processes.

One important note on employability skills: this term is often confused with processes and tools that are part of career coaching mechanisms, including interview skills, resume development, and general career search practices. We believe these elements are job search skills rather than employability skills. Further, we believe that employability skills require valid assessment as part of the overall evidence-based approach that is the foundation of this work.

Because of the evidence-based approach, the integration of employability skills in the classroom is appropriate and necessary for students seeking economic security through a progressive career pathway. As described in the previous chapter with foundational competencies, the integration of employability skills with curricula, both inside and outside of the classroom, is beginning to occur with early adopters in educational institutions around the country. Bringing these efforts to scale to serve more individuals and employers alike is a worthy goal, and one that this work can support.

Chapter 9 | Occupational Skills & Credentials

Occupational competencies are typically represented by credentials that are developed and maintained by professional organizations in the sector. The best credentialing organizations engage industrial psychologists to perform a job analysis that provides detailed occupational competency information that then becomes the basis for curriculum, accreditation, assessment, credentialing, and continuing education.

The major professional organizations in sectors like healthcare, law, and accounting tightly govern credentials that require alignment with both curricula and degrees (for example Registered Nurses, Attorneys, and Certified Public Accountants), but there is a lot of variation in credential quality among and within many sectors. This is most true in the market for entry-level and middle-skills credentials that has emerged in the last decade.

There are a number of people working to articulate ways to navigate and organize the credentialing landscape. We recommend looking at three sources in particular (all of which are easily available on-line):

- Lumina (2015), Connecting Credentials: A Beta Credentials Framework (a snapshot of this framework is included at the end of this chapter)
- Corporation for a Skilled Workforce (CSW) (2013), Making a Market for Competency Based Credentials
- Business Roundtable (2016), Credential Engine: Moving Credentialing Forward

From these and other like-minded efforts, certain common indicators of quality credentials have recently begun to emerge. Such indicators include the presence of a well-defined competency model, the use of assessments, the involvement of accreditation bodies, Continuing Education Unit requirements (CEUs), and others. When assessing a list of credentials, questions you can ask yourself include:

- Is the credential based on a professional job analysis?
- Did the developers work with a professional test development company?
- Are the developers working with an accreditation body?
- Are there CEUs?

The above data is available from the US DOL O*NET database for many credentials.

Based on our experience, we would list the following features as "ideal" characteristics of quality credentials:

- Unified governance over the professional organization ensures continuous improvement and efficacy.
- Longitudinal validation studies are used to quantify the value to society and stakeholders.
- Credentialing organizations conduct consortium-style job analysis and validation studies.
- Comprehensive job analysis is refreshed on a regular basis to ensure continuous improvement.
- Competency models detail occupational and foundational competencies with documented linkages.
- Emerging needs are managed professionally by the credentialing organization to vet need and ensure quality.
- The quality of the nation's workforce is paramount and drives the mission of the professional organization.
- Credentialing organizations have a tight focus and serve their members and stakeholders well.
- Longitudinal validation is used to quantify the value of quality talent to employers and policy makers.
- Curriculum, accreditation, credentials, and continuing education are independent and aligned.
- Clear career pathways with feeder occupations and next step occupations are defined.

- Credentials are in demand because the value is clear to employers, individuals, educators, and the public.

The following illustration is the Beta Credentials Framework.

8 LEVELS

The level requirements and competencies in study and work are described in terms of the degree of:
- Adaptability
- Complexity
- Range
- Selectivity

KNOWLEDGE

Knowledge describes what a learner knows, understands and can demonstrate in terms of the body of facts, principles, theories and practices related to fields of application (study and work). The requirements and competencies are described in terms of: • Depth • Breadth • Dimension

Level 1 Demonstrates achievement of fundamental competencies to complete narrow and limited tasks within a highly structured field of study or work under direct supervision or guidance.

- Demonstrates general knowledge within predetermined fields of study or work.

Level 2 Demonstrates achievement of fundamental competencies to complete technical, routine tasks within a structured field of study or work largely subject to overall direction or guidance.

- Demonstrates and uses basic knowledge within a field of study or work that includes relevant principles and practices.

Level 3 Demonstrates competencies for processing well-defined technical tasks that are less structured and include non-routine tasks. These tasks have some degree of complexity, assigned within a comprehensive field of study or occupational activity subject to some change and largely subject to overall supervision or guidance.

- Demonstrates and applies extended knowledge within a field of study or field of occupational activity.
- This includes the knowledge of a limited range of technical and theoretical concepts, procedures and solutions to predictable problems.

Level 4 Demonstrates competencies for the processing of specialized and complex tasks within a comprehensive field of study or an occupational environment that is subject to change. This requires theoretical knowledge and practical skills to select appropriate principles and procedures and may involve overall supervision.

- Demonstrates a comprehensive theoretical and technical knowledge within a field of study or an occupational field to determine solutions to unfamiliar patterns.

Level 5 Demonstrates advanced competencies for the processing of comprehensive tasks assigned within a complex and specialized field of study or occupational activity subject to change. This requires the ability to select and apply appropriate theoretical knowledge and practical skills to perform technical tasks in a broad range of contexts.

- Demonstrates integrated and specialized professional knowledge within a field of study or occupational activity.
- This includes deeper theoretical and professional knowledge, including the scope, the core theories and practices and the limitations of the field of study or field of occupational activity.

Level 6 Demonstrates mastery in the processing of comprehensive tasks and problems within subareas of a field of study or within a field of occupational activity characterized by a high degree of complexity and by frequent changes. This requires a high degree of theoretical knowledge and practical skills.

- Demonstrates broad integrated knowledge concerning scientific principles and the practical application of a scientific or complex subject.
- This includes a critical understanding of the most important theories, a range of methods as well as relevant and innovative occupational and technical developments to address complex problems.
- Demonstrates knowledge related to the further development of a scientific or complex subject, a field of occupational activity or relevant knowledge at the interface of different areas.

Level 7 Demonstrates competencies for the processing of new and complex professional tasks and problem settings within a scientific subject or an occupational field characterized by frequent and unpredictable changes. This requires the need to elucidate the major theories and the application of advanced specialized knowledge, research methods and approaches in various contexts.

- Demonstrates comprehensive, detailed, specialized and state-of-the-art knowledge in a scientific subject or in a strategically oriented field of professional activity.
- This includes demonstrating an extended knowledge in adjoining areas of study or work, major theories, methods and schools of practice in the field of study or profession, and their relationships to allied fields.

Level 8 Demonstrates competencies for obtaining research findings in a scientific subject or for the development of innovative solutions and procedures in highly complex and novel problem situations within a field of occupational activity. This requires a capacity for a wide range of strategic and scientific thinking and creative action.

- Demonstrates comprehensive, specialized, systematic state-of-the-art knowledge in a discipline or profession and contributes to innovation or the expansion of knowledge.
- This includes specialized knowledge at the interface of adjoining disciplines or areas of practice that may include the acquisition and application of knowledge in a new discipline or professional area.

SKILLS

Skills describe what an individual can do in applying knowledge, completing tasks, and solving problems (involving the use of logical, intuitive and creative thinking). Skills can be described in terms of types and complexity and include cognitive, technical, communication, interpersonal and practical skills (involving manual dexterity and the use of methods, materials, tools and instruments).

Specialized skills include occupational and discipline-specific skills.

Personal skills describe the competency required to act in an independent and responsible manner in various situations, to exercise judgment and demonstrate critical thinking and problem solving.

Social skills describe the individual's ability to demonstrate respect for the behavior of others and differing viewpoints, to communicate with others effectively, and to work effectively with people from diverse backgrounds and points of view.

SPECIALIZED SKILLS

The requirements and competencies are described in terms of:
- **Critical Thinking and Judgment**
- **Integrative Application**
- **Systems Thinking**

• Demonstrates basic cognitive and practical skills required to carry out tasks with stipulated rules.	• Demonstrates ability to recognize and to act on elementary relationships between assignments and tasks.
• Demonstrates basic cognitive and practical skills required to carry out tasks within a field of study or work.	• Evaluates the results of such tasks in accordance with pre-stipulated criteria and establishes correlations among functions and tasks.
• Demonstrates a broad range of cognitive and practical skills which facilitate autonomous preparation for performing tasks and problem solving, identifying and using relevant methods and skills to complete tasks and to address well-defined problems having a measure of complexity.	• Evaluates results in accordance with criteria which are largely pre-stipulated, provides simple reporting of methods and results.
• Demonstrates the use of a broad range of cognitive and practical skills which facilitate problem solving and the completion of complex tasks. • Plans and designs appropriate approaches and processes, evaluates work and learning results.	• Demonstrates ability to select alternative actions or practices based on observations of reciprocal effects on other functional areas or tasks.
• Demonstrates an extended, broad range of specialized cognitive and practical skills. • Identifies and frames complex problems in selected areas of study and work, and distinguishes among ideas, concepts, theories or practical approaches to solve those problems.	• Plans work processes across learning and work areas. Evaluates such processes, comprehensively considering alternatives and their potential impacts.
• Demonstrates and applies a comprehensive range of methods for processing complex tasks and problems within a scientific subject, field of study or field of professional activity. • Differentiates and evaluates theories and approaches to selected complex problems within the chosen field of study or professional activity.	• Develops and evaluates new solutions and considers the effect on various criteria even in circumstances where requirements are subject to frequent change.
• Demonstrates specialized technical or conceptual skills to analyze, consolidate and synthesize knowledge in order to identify and to provide solutions to strategic problems in a scientific subject or in a field of professional activity.	• This includes the initiation, planning and evaluation of varied specialized technical or creative functions, the exploration of current limits of theory, knowledge and practice, and the consideration of alternatives. • Demonstrates high-level, independent judgments in a range of technical or management functions and articulates significant challenges involved.
• Demonstrates and applies skills in making high-level, independent judgments in a range of technical or management functions in varied specialized contexts. This includes the initiation, planning and evaluation of broad specialized technical and creative functions comprising cross-activity areas and the consideration of alternatives.	• Demonstrates comprehensively developed skills for the identification and solution of novel problems set in the areas of research, development or innovation within a specialized scientific subject or in a field of professional activity.

Chapter 10 | Industry-Wide Skills & Credentials

Industry-wide skills and credentials describe and certify skills used in more than one job within an industry sector or segment of an industry. These are the skills that make it possible for employees to move easily across industry sub-sectors or along career paths within an industry. Developing industry-wide technical skills makes it possible for individuals to have opportunities for a variety of jobs.

States and regions across the country have the opportunity, and incentive, to create industry-wide credentials that are developed in concert with employers. As part of the 2014 Workforce Innovation and Opportunity Act (WIOA), industry-driven credentials are highly encouraged and seen as valuable tools for local labor markets and regional economies.

The proliferation of unique and locally-defined credentials is generally not helpful for individuals as they try to build stackable credentials within various industries. Unique credentials that can't translate from region to region are not helpful to the individual or to employers in general. However, regions adopting and then adapting industry-wide credentials that respond to the needs and proactively address short- and long-term workforce plans of local employers is a critical element for workforce agencies and educational institutions alike.

Industries across the country have developed some key industry-wide credentials, although these efforts have generally not reached scale in terms of the overall American workforce. Developing these kind of credentials in coordination with foundational and occupational credentials will help individuals build their overall stackable credential inventory.

Described below are a few industry-wide credentials that are in use or skill sets that have been developed. There are undoubtedly more that are used beyond

these examples, but these provide a basic snapshot of industry-wide credentials.

Manufacturing

- Manufacturing Skill Standards Council (MSSC) certifies essential Production modules in Safety, Quality Practices & Measurement, Manufacturing Processes & Production, and Maintenance Awareness.
- Manufacturing Skills Institute (MSI) offers certifications that address core industry-wide skills standards required for skilled production occupations in all sectors of manufacturing. The core competency areas certified include: (1) Math and Measurement, (2) Spatial Reasoning and Manufacturing Technology, and (3) Business Acumen and Quality.

Healthcare

- Health Professions Pathways (H2P core curriculum) provides industry-wide skills at the entry level focused on six different content areas that span a significant variety of healthcare career pathways. The six content areas are: (1) Basic Health Professions Skills I; (2) Wellness and Health Promotion; (3) General Health Professions Management; (4) Basic Health Professions II; (5) Pharmacology for Health Professions; and (6) Pathophysiology.
- Basic emergency and clinical certifications, including CPR, infection control, and medical waste handling.

Retail

- Retail Management Certification provided by the Western Association of Food Chains and offered at college campuses around the country.
- RISE UP Retail Industry Fundamentals
- NRF Customer Service and Sales
- NRF Advanced Customer Service and Sales

Chapter 11 | Occupational Credentials, Degrees, & Licenses

Certifications and licenses are credentials that demonstrate a level of skill or knowledge needed to perform a specific type of job. Certifications are issued by a non-governmental body (such as a professional organization), but licenses are awarded by a government agency and convey a legal authority to work in an occupation. People may have more than one certification or license; people with a license may also have a certification.

It's important to distinguish certifications and licenses from degrees awarded by educational institutions. In many cases, certifications and licenses require a degree, either an associates or bachelors, from an accredited institution. However, simply possessing a degree almost never confers upon the individual the specific certification and license. On one end of the spectrum, some certifications and licenses simply require a registration process. On the other end of the spectrum, an additional and comprehensive assessment process is required even after a degree is conferred. Lawyers and Certified Public Accountants are two professions that require significant assessment post-degree. And in the middle of this spectrum are certifications and licenses that don't necessarily require any degree but require a separate and distinct assessment.

The following information from the Bureau of Labor Statistics within the U.S. Department of Labor helps further illustrate the landscape of certifications and licenses:

- The occupations in which workers have the highest likelihood of having a certification or license are healthcare practitioners and technical occupations (76.9 percent), legal occupations (68.1 percent), and education, training, and library occupations (55.5 percent). In most fields,

licenses were the predominant credential.

- The occupation group with the highest likelihood of certification, but no license was computer and mathematical occupations, at 8.5 percent in 2015; this was also the only occupation where licenses were not the predominant credential.
- Government workers (which include many workers in education and health services) were more likely to hold a certification or license (40.6 percent) than private industry workers (22.6 percent).

Helping individuals understand the sometimes-complex circumstances surrounding certifications and licenses up front is essential. Post-secondary institutions often build the cost of sitting for a certification or licensure assessment into their overall program costs so that students can better plan and prepare. In cases where that doesn't happen, workforce agencies, community based organizations, career coaches, and any other individual or agency that works with individuals should adequately address the process for obtaining a certification or license early on.

Section IV

Evidence-Based Career Profiles

"The career profile is a comprehensive set of evidence that describes the aspirations, skills, competencies, and credentials of individuals seeking good jobs."

career profiles
evidence-based

ASSESSMENTS

Documenting skills within a profile provides a reliable attestation of individual qualifications.

REFERENCES & BACKGROUND

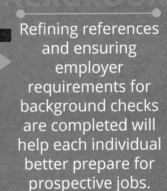

Refining references and ensuring employer requirements for background checks are completed will help each individual better prepare for prospective jobs.

STRUCTURED INTERVIEWS

Structured interviews help individuals better prepare for and represent themselves during interviews.

CAREER COACHING & PATHWAYS

Each profile should include documented career coaching and pathway elements that illustrate long-term goals.

RESUME, COVER LETTER, & STACKABLE CREDENTIALS

These traditional tools should document the skills, abilities, and credentials that an individual brings to prospective employers.

| Chapter 12 | Assembling the Career Profile |

Career profile Overview

The Career Profile is a comprehensive profile that describes the aspirations, skills, competencies, and credentials of individuals seeking good jobs.

This section describes the MRI recommendations for the Career Profile. We provide here a Career Profile framework that illustrates the concept with supporting details. The specific Profile content will need to be adapted for each job family to include specific elements related to the jobs in the job family. The specific employer use of the Profile will also need to be clarified and communicated. In this guide, we recommend that employers guarantee an interview for individuals with a Career Profile and a recommendation from a designated community partner. Our illustration is based on this recommendation.

The "guaranteed interview" is included in our recommendation for two reasons. First, it provides a helpful incentive to individuals to complete a career profile. Individuals will have the assurance that they will get through the automated screening steps included in many of the sophisticated applicant tracking systems (ATS) in use by employers. Second, it helps get the best candidates in front of recruiters. Automated screening methods, such as knock-out questions and ranking questions may be confusing to applicants for entry-level jobs. This may cause the system to automatically reject applicants that might in fact be good workers. The career profile, along with a reliable reference from

a community partner, will help ensure that the best candidates get to the recruiters.

The career profile includes essential elements that each individual must complete, with the help of a community partner if needed. The process is designed to help individuals better position themselves for jobs with local employers. As part of the career coaching process, individuals will have completed cognitive and personality assessments with the local backbone support organization. Many of these same assessments are used in the career profile. If the individual participates in lengthy education and training experiences, the assessments should be repeated to enable the candidate to document the newly acquired skills. These evidence-based methods help ensure that individuals who seek jobs through the career profile process have the appropriate job-related skills and meet all of the essential job qualifications. The career profile provides employers with assurance of the quality of candidates.

This career profile process will utilize the following best and leading practices in order to accomplish the following goals:

1. Qualified individuals who complete the career profile in totality will be guaranteed an interview for open positions they are qualified for with at least one engaged employer.
2. Organizations and community partners that are part of this initiative will share data in a way that better positions the individual to be competitively considered for open positions, and that better serves the broader workforce within the region.
3. Employers will develop long-term workforce plans based on the Career Navigation System model and leverage the energy and resources of community organizations to build robust talent supply chains.

Career Profile Elements

Resume & Cover Letter – individuals develop a traditional resume and cover letter.

Reference Development – individuals develop a list of five references that can describe their work and/or educational history, skills, values, and relevant

attributes for the job they are seeking.

Release Forms – individuals will complete necessary release forms so that important data can be shared among relevant partners to ensure progress, effectiveness, and success of the individual, while still maintaining confidentiality.

Background Checks – individuals will complete background checks with their community partner to ensure that they are able to compete for open positions, based on requirements for various sectors. This action step is intended to ensure that each individual has the information they need to make important decisions about participating in this process. These background checks are not shared with employers.

Computer Proficiency – individuals will complete a locally-designated computer proficiency test to ensure they meet minimum standards for successfully using technology in the workplace.

Foundational Skill Assessments – as part of the career coaching process, individuals will complete foundational assessments in order to document their ability to compete for jobs in their region.

Structured Interview Practice – individuals participate in a practice structured interview with the backbone support organization or other community based organization in order to simulate the experience of a real structured interview, a process that can be daunting even for the most experienced individual.

As previously discussed, additional elements can, and most likely will, be added to a region's local career profile based on specific occupational requirements and/or employer requirements beyond these basic elements. In all cases, with these and any additional elements, the career profile should be developed and used as an inclusive tool that invites diverse and qualified candidates to be considered for open positions. This tool has been designed to be inclusive in that manner and should be used so accordingly.

Chapter 13 | The Use of Assessments in Career Profiles

Cognitive and Personality Assessments

As described in Chapters 4 and 5, cognitive and personality assessments are a key part of the evidence-based career coaching process. They were presented there as the essential first step in which participants develop the self-awareness that will allow them to define their possible job paths and guide education and training plans.

In the career profile, by contrast, assessments are a signal to potential employers of the competencies that a candidate possesses. Depending on the kind of test, employers can verify minimum requirements of the job, or they can use them simply as one piece of evidence among many others that help determine a candidate's strengths, weaknesses, and overall fit within the organization.

We provide two tests from ETS as examples:

ETS WorkFORCE Assessment for Cognitive Ability measures basic cognitive skills in Reading Prose, Reading Documents, and Quantitative abilities. This test is designed to measure the abilities needed for a particular position employers are seeking to fill, and can be used in the hiring process in various industries when considering new employees for targeted positions or within training programs designed to help prepare individuals for targeted positions.

ETS WorkFORCE Assessment for Job Fit helps identify candidates that are most likely to succeed in a particular job and organization by measuring how well a candidate's behavioral skills fit the requirement of a specific job. The

assessment measures six behavioral competencies and 13 underlying behavioral attributes that are known to be predictive of workplace performance. The test provides employers with an Expected Job Fit Indicator that indicates the candidate's likelihood of success in the position the employer is seeking to fill. The score is therefore tailored to the type of job the employer is filling and the behavioral skills candidates need to perform successfully in that job. Working with employers, career coaches and caseworkers should have some idea of which candidates scores may make them a good fit for a partner employer.

The inclusion of assessment scores in the career profile provides valuable evidence-based information to partner employers.

Practice Session for a Structured Interview

Structured (or behavioral) interviews can be challenging parts of the job search process for anyone, regardless of experience or the level of the job. For many individuals, a structured interview might be a brand new concept – candidates expecting a casual conversation might be surprised by the direct, rigorous questions that can seem a bit like an interrogation. Behavioral questions, like those used in structured interviews, are designed to provoke descriptions of the past behavior of the candidate in a circumstance that demonstrates a relevant competency. The idea is that past behavior is the best predictor of future behavior.

Accordingly, the career navigation process includes a structured interview practice session. The results of the interview are for practice purposes only. Similarly, participants should be aware that the questions asked in the practice session are not likely to be the same that individual employers will ask.

The structured interview is a process that should remain confidential; the results of the interview should never be shared with the employer so that it does not create undue bias in one direction or another. Instead, the interview should be treated as a tool that community partners use with their participants in order to best prepare them for real interviews once they finish the career profile. The following instructions are written for a coach to deliver an interview. Following the steps outlined in this process will ensure that job seekers are as prepared for a structured interview as possible.

Opening the Interview:

- Greet Candidate; put him/her at ease and establish tone of interview.
- Introduce Interviewer(s). Mention each interviewer's position in the organization.
- Explain purpose of interview:
    - To gather information to enable fair decision making.
    - To help candidate understand the organization and position.
- Explain that interviewer(s) will be taking notes during interview.
- Note: Any questions the candidate has regarding the organization or employment should be saved for the end of the interview to avoid bias in scoring.

Conducting the Interview:

- Read the first question verbatim.
- Take very thorough and objective notes on the candidate's answer.
    - For each question, you are seeking a complete description of a critical Incident involving the competency, the Actions the candidate took in that incident, and the Outcome of the incident.
    - Use the appropriate probes when necessary to ensure complete understanding of the candidate's description of the incident (I), actions (A) and outcome (O) for each question.
    - Record as much information about the behavior reported by the candidate as possible.
- Repeat for all questions.
- Note: Reading all questions verbatim to the candidate ensures the reliability of the selection process and its fairness to all job candidates. DO NOT interpret the questions for the candidate, as it may unfairly lead them to a particular answer. DO allow the candidate to take a moment to reflect on the question if necessary.

Closing the Interview:

- Conclude the interview. Inform the candidate of next steps in the employment process.

- Do not tell the candidate anything about his or her performance during the interview.
- Solicit any questions the candidate may have about employment or the organization.
- Thank the candidate for their participation in the interview and interest in your organization.

Post Interview – Evaluation:

- After the interview is completed, review your notes and enter the score on the Summary Form that best represents the candidate's answer. As your guide, use the anchors provided and the response notes that you took.
- The interviewer should make ratings for each response individually.
- Calculate average scores for the candidate by adding the scores on the Summary Form together and dividing by the number of questions.
- Record any additional comments about the interview/candidate in the given section on the Summary Form.
- Keep all notes and forms for documentation.

Rating Scale Rubric

5 **Ideal**	Expert candidate. Can apply the competency in exceptionally difficult situations. Candidate has served as a key resource and advised others. Ideal answer.
4 **Advanced**	Exceeds standards. Can apply the competency in considerably difficult situations. Candidate requires no guidance.
3 **Average**	Meets standards. Can apply the competency in difficult situations. Candidate may require occasional guidance. Average answer.
2 **Basic**	Approaching standards. Can apply the competency in somewhat difficult situations. Candidate will require frequent guidance.
1 **Aware**	Limited awareness of standards. Can apply the competency in the simplest situation. Candidate requires close and extensive guidance.

Question 1 - Customer Service Orientation

Tell me about a time when you went beyond a customer's expectations.

       Incident: What was the situation?

       Action: What did you do that exceeded the customer's expectations?

       Outcome: What was the result?

Candidate Response:

_____

_____

_____

_____

_____

_____

_____

_____

_____

_____

_____

_____

_____

_____

_____

_____

_____

_____

Question 2 - Teamwork

Tell me about a time when you abandoned your personal needs or objectives in order to help the team.

  Incident: What was the situation your team was in?
  Action: What did you do to help the team rather than yourself?
  Outcome: What did you learn from this experience?

Candidate Response:

_____

_____

_____

_____

_____

_____

_____

_____

_____

_____

_____

_____

_____

_____

_____

_____

_____

_____

Question 3 - Time Management

Tell me about a time when you felt like you had too much to do and not enough time to do it.

Incident: How did you end up in that situation?

Action: What did you do to get as much done as possible?

Outcome: What was the outcome?

Candidate Response:

_____

_____

_____

_____

_____

_____

_____

_____

_____

_____

_____

_____

_____

_____

_____

_____

Question 4 - Critical Thinking and Problem Solving

Tell me about a decision you have made that could have had serious consequences if you were wrong.

Incident:	What was the decision you had to make?
Action:	How did you think through what to do?
Outcome:	How did it turn out, and what did you learn?

Candidate Response:

_____

_____

_____

_____

_____

_____

_____

_____

_____

_____

_____

_____

_____

_____

_____

_____

_____

_____

Chapter 14 | Career Profile Outputs

A complete Career Profile will consist of the following elements:

1. Resume and Cover Letter
2. References
3. Release Forms
4. Attestation of Computer Proficiency
5. Foundational Assessment Scores
6. Career Pathway MAP: My Action Plan

Note that while background checks are performed for each individual to inform coaching and pathway development, these checks are strictly confidential and not included in the Career Profile. Further, some states and/or localities may have laws that govern how background checks can be performed, even if not shared with an employer. Local practitioners should engage in robust conversation about this topic, as necessary, to ensure this process follows the law while also serving the interests of the individual.

The Career Profile submission form on the next page will be used for each individual seeking a job through this process. This form is a one-page glance at the comprehensive career profile and will be filled out by the individual, community partners, and the backbone support organization before submitting to the employer. Only the designated backbone support organization can submit the form to an employer, and the backbone organization will conduct final quality checks on each of the profile items to ensure that an individual is ready for an interview.

Career Profile Submission Form

Name: _____

Email: _____

Phone: _____

Community Partner: _____

Name: _____

Email: _____

Phone: _____

#1 Resume & Cover Letter
(Submit as Attachment)

#2 Reference Check Preparation
(Submit as Attachment)

#3 Career Coaching & Pathway Development
(Submit as Attachment)

#4 Structured Interview Practice Completed _____ _____
YES   NO

#5 Release Form
(Submit as Attachment)

#6 Background Check _____ _____
YES   NO

#7 Computer Proficiency
(As defined by specific job) _____ _____
YES   NO

#8 Assessment
(Include Scores) _____ _____ _____
Prose   Doc   Quant

#9 Training Assessment
(Brief Description) _____
_____

To be completed by backbone support organization:

WorkFORCE Assessment for Cognitive Ability Scores			WorkFORCE Assessment for Job Fit Score	
Prose	Doc	Quant		Indicator

Applying For _____

Previous Employment/ Application History _____
_____

Date of Submission: _____   Phone: _____

Name: _____   Email: _____

Sections Completed: 1 ___ 2 ___ 3 ___ 4 ___ 5 ___ 6 ___ 7 ___ 8 ___ 9 ___

1. Resume & Cover Letter

A resume and cover letter should be developed following normal standards for both documents. As part of this process, the individual should learn how to adapt both the resume and cover letter for a specific job opportunity. These should be submitted with the Career Profile as attachments.

2. Reference Building

As part of the career profile process, individuals will need to identify at least five references that can describe their academic, professional, and personal attributes. The references will not be contacted during the career profile process. Instead, developing this list, including contact information, early on in the process will help speed up the selection process if an offer of employment is made. Often times, individuals don't have contact information readily available and that can significantly delay the on-boarding process, and ultimately hurt both the individual and the employer.

This form is meant to assist in collecting the information needed for formal reference checks that occur as part of the interview process. Completing this form does not initiate the reference checking process. At least two references must be a professional or managerial reference, as described below. References should not be a friend or family member.

Professional Reference Examples: Manager, Supervisor, Team Lead. If limited or no work history, then Volunteer Coordinator, Clinical Instructor, Teacher, Mentors or Clergy/Faith-based Leaders may serve as references.

Professional Reference	
Reference Name	
Reference Company	
Reference Job Title	
Reference Phone Number	
Reference Email	
Relationship to Candidate	
Dates Worked Together	

Personal Reference Examples: Colleague, Coworker, Classmate

Personal Reference	
Reference Name	
Reference Company	
Reference Job Title	
Reference Phone Number	
Reference Email	
Relationship to Candidate	
Dates Worked Together	

3. Release Forms

In each region, the backbone support organization will manage the various forms required so that appropriate levels of data sharing can occur. At least two primary forms for the release of information will be required: (1) authorization to release information between the employer and the backbone support organization; and (2) authorization to release information between the backbone support organization and each of the local community partners. These forms will vary from region to region, as well as the type of data that is shared. The sharing of information is designed to better facilitate support for the individual seeking a career, program improvement over time, and general assessment of the efficacy of the program region by region. Because state and federal law does not allow for release of information, nor do most employers' internal policies, these forms are critical and required for organized, regional efforts.

4. Attestation of Computer Proficiency

Regional specifications for the career profile will dictate how computer proficiency should be documented and shared. For many positions, a simple attestation of Yes or No on the Career profile Submission Form will suffice. If more documentation is needed, that decision can be made locally.

5. Foundational Assessment Scores

Foundational Assessment Scores should be noted on the Career Profile

Submission Form. Whenever possible, certificates or transcripts that are produced as a result of foundational assessments should be included as attachments with the Career Profile as well.

6. Career Pathway MAP: My Action Plan

As discussed in chapter 4, a central component of the career profile process is the development of a comprehensive career pathway, which contains the following elements, each of which will have been gathered during the four-step career coaching process:

- Career Aspirations – an outline of what specific careers an individual seeks to pursue.
- Training & Credential Requirements – an outline of specific training and credentials needed to meet the requirements for stated career aspirations.
- Supportive Services – an outline of the necessary supportive services that will enable an individual's success in securing and maintaining a long-term career.

A filled-out template can be used as part of the interview process with employers, just as resumes and cover letters are used. The graphic representation of a career pathway can be a more impactful representation of one's aspirations compared to a written narrative.

Once the form is filled out, the individual should be able to see and understand the progression of their career plan. In addition, the individual should be able to describe what specific needs they have at the beginning of their pathway, and how those needs can be reduced as they progress through their path. For instance, if transportation is needed for Job 1, an individual should be able to see that progression on this pathway will mean that the issue of transportation can and needs to be solved as they progress to Job 2 or Job 3. This form should be informative as well as encouraging for the individual.

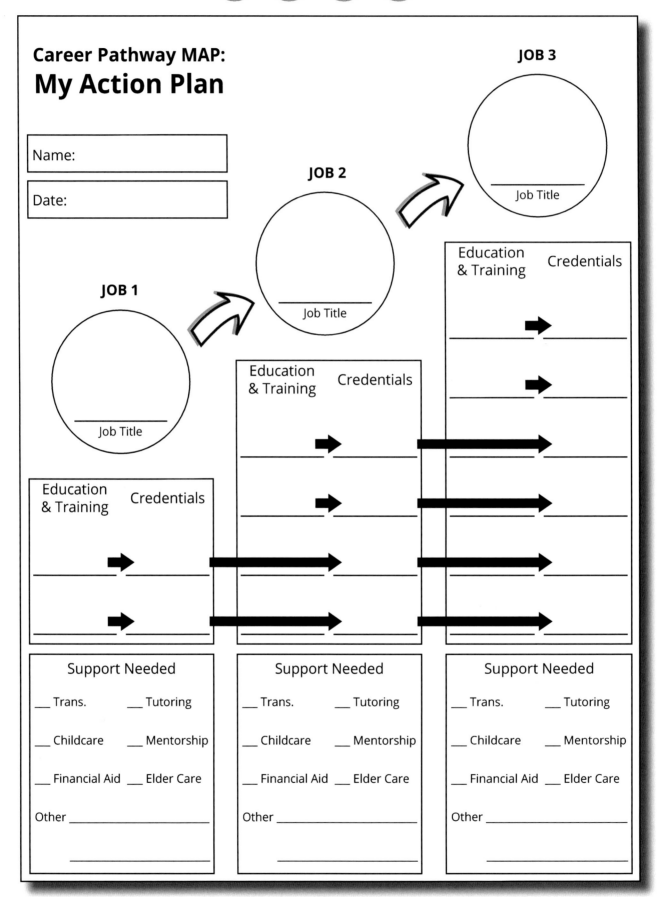

Career Pathway MAP:
My Action Plan

Name:

Date:

JOB 3

Job Title

JOB 2

Job Title

JOB 1

Job Title

Education & Training   Credentials

Education & Training   Credentials

Education & Training   Credentials

Support Needed

__ Trans.   __ Tutoring

__ Childcare   __ Mentorship

__ Financial Aid   __ Elder Care

Other _____

_____

Support Needed

__ Trans.   __ Tutoring

__ Childcare   __ Mentorship

__ Financial Aid   __ Elder Care

Other _____

_____

Support Needed

__ Trans.   __ Tutoring

__ Childcare   __ Mentorship

__ Financial Aid   __ Elder Care

Other _____

_____

WorkFORCE. — *Measuring the Power of Learning.*

Certificate of Achievement

This is to certify that

Name Longname

achieved the following scores for the

WorkFORCE **Assessment for Cognitive Ability**

Reading Prose XXX of a possible 500
Reading Documents XXX of a possible 500
Quantitative XXX of a possible 500

Date Month / day / year

Visit **www.ets.org/workforce** or review your score report for details about levels.

David L. Hunt
David L. Hunt
Senior Vice President
Global Education and Workforce Division, ETS

WorkFORCE. — *Measuring the Power of Learning.*

Certificate of Achievement

Awarded to

for successfully completing the
WorkFORCE Readiness Training Program

WorkFORCE. ASSESSMENT FOR DEVELOPMENT

Section V

Appendices

A: Glossary
Our most commonly used terms, with definitions pulled from multiple sources, as noted.

B: Sources and Recommendations
Our compilation of sources and recommendations that have informed our thinking about this work, as referenced in the "Dig Deeper" section of many of the chapters throughout this book.

C: Joint Letter on Career Pathways (2016)
An important, updated letter from over a dozen federal agencies supporting the national movement focusing on career pathways as a means for building a world-class workforce system.

D: ETS WorkFORCE Assessment for Cognitive Ability

E: ETS WorkFORCE Assessment for Job Fit

F: ETS WorkFORCE Assessment for Career Development

Appendix A

Glossary

Definitions marked with an asterisk are taken from the DOL Career Pathways Toolkit (DOL 2011); definitions marked with a double asterisk are taken from Shared Vision, Strong Systems (CLASP/AQCP 2014).

Abilities: Enduring attributes of the individual that influence performance. O*NET ability statements refer to the power to perform an observable activity at the present time. This means that abilities have been evidenced through activities or behaviors that are similar to those required on the job, e.g., ability to plan and organize work.

*Apprenticeship: Apprenticeship is a combination of on-the-job training and related instruction in which workers learn the practical and theoretical aspects of a highly skilled occupation. Apprenticeship programs can be sponsored by individual employers, joint employer and labor groups, and/or employer associations. The Department of Labor's role is to safeguard the welfare of apprentices, ensure equality of access to apprenticeship programs, and provide integrated employment and training information to sponsors and the local employment and training community.

*Assessment: The use of standardized instruments, interviews, or other means to determine factors that may contribute to the success of students in career and technology programs. These factors may include interest, aptitude, academic achievement, work experience, learning style, work values, and other traits. Assessment may also be administered to determine progress attained by students during training or areas of need to address through remediation.

**Assessment: The process of gathering and documenting information about the achievement, skills, abilities, and personality variables of an individual. The process and tools used for the assessment must be reliable, valid, and diagnostic and must be used appropriately to place individuals in educational levels and programs and measure their progress.

Career coaching: Career coaching is a discipline that involves two distinct functions: coaching and counseling. The purpose is to help people make informed decisions about their career development and trajectory, as well as to identify the tools and services that they need to meet their goals.

Career navigation assistance: Services that assist participants in determining a career path, understanding the requirements for the jobs they seek, and accessing the education and training needed to achieve their goals.

Career Pathway: A career pathway is an integrated collection of programs and services intended to develop students' core academic, technical and employability skills; and to provide them with continuous education, training, and placement in high-demand, high-opportunity jobs.

*Career Pathways:** The term "career pathway" means a combination of rigorous and high-quality education, training, and other services that:

- Aligns with the skill needs of industries in the economy of the state or regional economy involved;
- Prepares an individual to be successful in any of a full range of secondary or postsecondary education options, including registered apprenticeships;
- Includes counseling to support an individual in achieving the individual's education and career goals;
- Includes, as appropriate, education offered concurrently with and in the same context as workforce preparation activities and training for a specific occupation or occupational cluster;
- Organizes education, training, and other services to meet the particular needs of an individual in a manner that accelerates the educational and career advancement of the individual to the extent practicable;
- Enables an individual to attain a secondary school diploma or its recognized equivalent and at least one recognized postsecondary credential; and
- Helps an individual enter or advance within a specific occupation or occupational cluster.

Career Pathways: An operationalization of the career pathway approach that includes three essential features: (1) well-connected and transparent education, training, credential, and support service offerings within specific sectors or cross-sector occupations (often delivered via multiple linked and aligned programs); (2) multiple entry points that enable well-prepared students as well as targeted populations with limited education, skills, English, and work experiences to successfully enter the career pathway (targeted populations served by career pathways may include adult education or other lower-skilled adult students, English language learners, offenders or ex-offenders, certain high school students; disconnected or "opportunity" youth, former military personal, un- or under-employed adults, or others); and (3) multiple exit points at successively higher levels leading to self- or family-supporting employment and aligned with subsequent entry points. Career pathways also include four essential functions: (a) participant-focused education and training; (b) consistent and non-duplicative assessments of participants' education, skills, and assets/needs; (c) support services and career navigation assistance to facilitate transitions; and (d) employment services and work experiences.

Career pathway system: The cohesive combination of partnerships, resources and funding, policies, data, and shared accountability measures that support the development, quality, scaling, and dynamic sustainability of career pathways and programs for youth and adults.

Career Technical Education (CTE): Career and technical education is a term applied to schools, institutions, and educational programs that specialize in career-focused programs that prepare students both for college and careers. Career and technical education programs offer both academic and career-oriented courses, and many provide students with the opportunity to gain work experience through work-based learning, such as internships, on-the-job training, and industry-certification opportunities. Career and technical education programs provide a wide range of learning experiences spanning many different career fields and industry sectors. Career and technical education may be offered in middle schools, high schools, vocational-technical schools, or through community colleges and other postsecondary institutions and certification programs.

Character Competencies: Soft skills, behavioral skills, personality factors.

CIP: Classification of Instructional Programs.

Cognitive Competencies: Mental processing skills.

Competency: A set of defined behaviors that provide a structured guide enabling the identification, evaluation, and development of the behaviors in individual employees. Competencies describe the capability to apply or use a set

of related knowledge, skills, and abilities required to successfully perform critical work functions or tasks in a defined work setting.

Competency-Based: Indicates that the decision is based on or has integrated the assessment of competency rather than some other method. Example: Competency-based education (CBE) awards credits based on mastery of competencies rather than time-in-seats.

**Competency-Based Credentialing: Model or method of awarding credit that uses defined learning outcomes and competencies instead of measuring learning through clock or credit hours.

*Competency-Based Curriculum: A program of study based on competency models that identify the knowledge, skills, and abilities necessary to successfully perform critical work functions in an industry or occupation.

Competency Validation: The process of defining competencies that are measurably related to job performance as well as gathering, organizing, and documenting evidence to substantiate the relationships.

**Credential: an attestation of qualification or competence issued to an individual by a third party (such as an educational institution or an industry or occupational certifying organization) with the relevant authority or assumed competence to issue such a credential. A credential is awarded in recognition of an individual's attainment of measurable technical or occupational skills necessary to obtain employment or advance within an occupation. These technical or occupational skills are generally based on standards developed or endorsed by employers. Credentials include degrees, diplomas, certificates, certifications, and licenses.

*Credentials: There are many different types of credentials offered or awarded by various types of organizations. Within the context of education, workforce development, and employment and training for the labor market, the term credential refers to a verification of qualification or competence issued to an individual by a third party with the relevant authority or jurisdiction to issue such credentials (such as an accredited educational institution, an industry-recognized association, or an occupational association or professional society).

The range of different types of credentials includes:
- Educational diplomas, certificates, and degrees;

- Registered apprenticeship certificates;
- Occupational licenses (typically awarded by state government agencies);
- Personnel certifications from industry or professional associations; and
- Other skill certificates for specific skill sets or competencies within one or more industries or occupations (e.g., writing, leadership, etc.).

Demand-driven: Demand-driven refers to an economic system that is organized according to consumer demand. In our case, it refers to the demand of employers for talent supplied by educators and workforce training organizations. We call on employer leadership to use evidence-based methods to define the competencies required for the jobs they need to fill. Employers need to clearly define jobs, the annual hiring rates by job and job family, and the competencies that are related to job performance for those jobs. Quality is defined as conformance to specifications. The first step to build a quality workforce is to gather clear specifications from employers.

**Disconnected youth: A low-income 16- to 24-year- old who also meets one or more of the following: has dropped out of high school; is within the age for compulsory school attendance but is over-age and under-credited (has not attended school for at least the most recent complete school year calendar quarter); has been subject to the juvenile or adult justice system or ordered by a court to an alternative school; is homeless/a runaway or under the care of the child welfare system; is pregnant or parenting and is not attending any school; has a disability; or is an English language learner. This term is also synonymous with the newer term, Opportunity Youth.

**Employment services: Services provided to participants that are designed to increase the employability of the un- or underemployed, which can include employment counseling, assistance with resume writing, mock interviews, job fairs, assistance with finding a job, and other similar services.

**Evidence-based practices or processes: Practices or processes of demonstrated effectiveness as shown by theoretical knowledge, practice data, program evaluation results, implementation data, and/or synthesis research

Evidence Based Selection Process (EBSP): Evidence-based selection processes use data on candidate competencies to manage the talent acquisition "pipeline" from a large pool of potential candidates to final hires. Key steps in this pipeline are sourcing, screening, selection, hiring and on-boarding. Competencies that have been determined to correlate to job performance through job analysis and validation studies are measured via cognitive assessments, character assessments, reference checks, and structured interview guides (SIGs) with behaviorally anchored rating scales (BARS).

*Fast-Track Programs: Fast-Track programs are accelerated programs that allow non-traditional learners to pace themselves according to their time availability and skill level. Fast-Track programs are designed to learn basic skills like literacy and math in the context of their career interest, making learning more relevant. Fast-Track programs are paced to meet the time commitments of non-traditional learners and may be offered on different schedules than conventional courses, thereby addressing their barriers to attending traditional course schedules. The goal of any Fast-Track program is for the learner to obtain some type of industry-recognized credential.

Foundational Competencies: Cognitive, Character and Physical competencies.

Industry: A specific grouping of companies with highly similar business activities within a sector. For example, the financial sector can be broken down into industries such as asset management, life insurance, and banking. Despite their differences in scope, the terms industry and sector are often incorrectly used interchangeably.

*Industry or Sector Partnership: A workforce collaborative convened by or acting in partnership with a state board or local board that:

- Organizes key stakeholders in an industry cluster into a working group that focuses on the shared goals and human resources needs of the industry cluster and that includes, at the appropriate stage of development of the partnership, a broad base of representatives including businesses, institutions of higher education, representatives of government, workforce agencies, labor organizations, and workforce boards.
- May also include representatives of state or local government; state or local boards, state or local economic development agencies, state workforce agency other state or local agencies, business or trade associations, economic development organizations, nonprofit organizations, community-based organizations, philanthropic organizations, and industry associations.

*Industry-recognized Credentials: An industry-recognized credential is one that either is developed and offered by, or endorsed by a nationally recognized industry association or organization representing a sizable portion of the industry sector, or a credential that is sought or accepted by companies within the industry sector for purposes of hiring or recruitment, which may include credentials from vendors of certain products. Consumer should be aware that in some industry sectors there may be more than one major industry association and that they may endorse or promote different credentials, and that the credentials that are sought by individual companies in an industry can vary by geographic region, by company size, or based on what product or equipment the company uses and needs workers to be able to operate. This is merely to point out that there may not be a single readily identifiable national credential for all industry sectors or occupations.

Job Analysis: The process of grouping jobs into a job family; analyzing the knowledge, skills, abilities, and work styles required to perform tasks in the job family; observing job functions via job shadows; and working with SMEs to evaluate the importance level of each competency related to performing the job.

Job Family: A group of jobs defined by a set of similar O*NET occupation codes that perform similar tasks and require similar competencies (knowledge, skills abilities and work-styles).

Job Shadow: An activity performed as part of job analysis in which analysts follow a worker to observe the work behaviors (tasks), tools, and technology used to perform the job.

Job Taxonomy: Specific jobs can be organized in a taxonomy. The Bureau of Labor Statistics (BLS) utilizes the Standard Occupational Classification (SOC) System to organize jobs into a four-level taxonomy of: major groups, minor groups, broad occupations, and detailed occupations. The O*NET begins with SOC codes and adds a 5th layer in the taxonomy by adding two decimal digits to the end of the SOC code. Employers can use the job taxonomy to organize job codes into coherent groups for validation studies.

JOFI: JOFI, short for Job Fit, is a trademark of Metrics Reporting, Inc. The JOFI foundational competency framework was developed for Metrics Reporting's job fit product (www.jofiscore.com).

Knowledge: Organized sets of principles and facts applying in general domains. O*NET Knowledge statements refer to an organized body of information (usually of a factual or procedural nature) which, if applied, makes adequate performance on the job possible. Each knowledge statement discusses a separate body of information applied directly to the performance of a function.

Key Performance Indicators: A measurable value that demonstrates how effectively an organization is achieving key business objectives. Organizations can use KPIs at multiple levels to evaluate their success at reaching targets.

**Labor market intelligence (LMI): Data and other information that can be used to understand labor market conditions in a particular region or local area. This can include employment statistics, unemployment rates and unemployment insurance claims, wages and salaries, job projections, and qualitative intelligence from employers.

Middle Skills Jobs: jobs that require education beyond high-school but short of a four year degree.

Occupational Competencies: specific job tasks and work activities that are specific to particular job families.

O*NET: The O*NET program is the U.S. Department of Labor's primary source of occupational information. The O*NET database contains information on hundreds of standardized and occupation-specific descriptors. Developed by Department of Labor.

Opportunity Youth: A new term synonymous with the "Disconnected Youth" definition.

*Portable Credential: A credential is considered portable when it is recognized and accepted as verifying the qualifications of an individual in other settings – either in other geographic areas, at other educational institutions, or by other industries or employing companies.

*Return on Investment (ROI): As it relates to career pathways, ROI is a measure of the net economic impact of an employment and training program. The ROI considers all the costs associated with design and implementation of the career pathway program, including costs to the participant, and compares the sum of those costs to the economic benefits achieved by all participants upon exiting the program and/or over time.

Sector: One of approximately 12 large segments in the economy. Despite their differences in scope, the terms industry and sector are often incorrectly used interchangeably.

Sector initiatives: Regional, industry-focused approaches to workforce and economic development that improve access to good jobs and/or increase job quality in ways that strengthen an industry's workforce.

*Sector Strategies:** Regional, industry-focused approaches to workforce and economic development that improve access to good jobs and increase job quality in ways that strengthen an industry's workforce. Although not a new approach, it is gaining national momentum as a proven framework for addressing skill gaps and engaging industry in education and training. The new Workforce Innovation and Opportunity Act (WIOA) makes significant changes to the nation's workforce development system, expressly incorporating the sector strategies approach throughout and requiring regional planning and alignment with local labor market needs for in-demand sectors and occupations.

Skills: Developed capacities that facilitate learning or the more rapid acquisition of knowledge. O*NET Skill statements refer to the proficient manual, verbal or mental manipulation of data or things. Skills an be readily measured by a performance test where quantity and quality of performance are tested, usually within an established time limit.

Standard Occupational Classification (SOC): The system of job codes developed by the Bureau of Labor Statistics.

Stackable Credentials: a credential that is a part of a sequence of credentials that can be accumulated over time to build individuals' qualifications and help them move along a career pathway or up a career ladder to different or potentially higher paying jobs.

*Stackable Credential:** A credential is considered stackable when it is part of a sequence of credentials that can be accumulated over time to build up an individual's qualifications and help them to move along a career pathway or up a career ladder to different and potentially higher-paying jobs. For example, one can stack a high school diploma, an associate degree, and then typically obtain two more years of appropriate postsecondary education to obtain a bachelor's degree. An individual can also stack an interim career/work readiness or pre-apprenticeship certificate, then complete an apprenticeship, and later earn a degree or advanced certification.

Subject Matter Expert (SME): An incumbent working in the job family or a manager with extensive job knowledge whose role is to help facilitators identify and prioritize tasks, knowledge, skills, abilities, and work styles important to performance in the job family.

Support services: The range of supports that should be available to students to help them persist in and complete their education or training program. These can include financial stability support, personal support, academic support, and career preparation support.

Talent Supply Chain Management (Talent SCM): Talent supply chain management is the application of supply chain management principles to the supply of talent. Talent SCM is a sourcing strategy that is well suited to solving talent shortages.

Tasks: Work behaviors; elements of a job. The things an individual does to perform a job.

Task Families: Groups of related tasks used for job analysis.

Validation: Defining competencies, and demonstrating that they are measurably related to job performance in accordance with Industrial and Organizational Psychology professional principles and standards.

Validity Generalization: An application of meta-analysis to the correlations between an employment test and a criterion, typically job or workplace training performance.

*Workforce Innovation and Opportunity Act (WIOA): The Federal statute that establishes Federal policy direction and appropriates Federal funds for employment and training programs. WIOA is designed to help job seekers access employment, education, training, and support services to succeed in the labor market and to match employers with the skilled workers they need to compete in the global economy. WIOA was signed into law on July 22, 2014. WIOA brings together, in strategic coordination, the core programs of Federal investment in skill development:

- Employment and training services for adults, dislocated workers, and youth and Wagner-Peyser employment services administered by the Department of Labor (DOL) through formula grants to states; and
- Adult education and literacy programs and vocational rehabilitation state grant programs that assist individuals with disabilities in obtaining employment administered by the Department of Education (ED).

WIOA also authorizes programs for specific vulnerable populations, including the Job Corps, YouthBuild, Indian and Native Americans, and Migrant and Seasonal Farmworker programs as well as evaluation and multi-state projects administered by DOL. In addition, WIOA authorizes other programs administered by ED and the Department of Health and Human Services. WIOA replaces the Workforce Investment Act of 1998 and retains and amends the Adult Education and Family Literacy Act, the Wagner-Peyser Act, and the Rehabilitation Act of 1973.

Appendix B

Sources and Recommendations

ACT (2011). Breaking New Ground: Building a National Workforce Skills Credentialing System. Iowa City, IA: ACT Workforce Development Division. Retrieved from: https://act.org/research/policymakers/pdf/BreakingNewGround.pdf

Adelman, C., Ewell, P., Gaston, P., & Schneider, C. G. (2011). The Degree Qualifications Profile. Defining Degrees: A New Direction for American Higher Education to Be Tested and Developed in Partnership with Faculty, Students, Leaders and Stakeholders. Lumina Foundation for Education.

Alliance for Quality Career Pathways (AQCP). (2014). Shared vision, strong systems: the Alliance for Quality Career Pathways Framework version 1.0. Retrieved from: http://www.clasp.org/issues/postsecondary/pages/aqcp-framework-version-1-0

American Educational Research Association (AERA), American Psychological Association (APA), National Council on Measurement in Education (NCME) (2014). The Standards for Educational and Psychological Testing. Washington D.C.: AERA Publishing.

Bird, K., Foster, M., & Ganzglass, E. (2014). New opportunities to improve economic and career success for low-income youth and adults: Key provisions of the Workforce Innovation and Opportunity Act (WIOA). Washington, DC: Center for Law and Social Policy.

Carnevale, A. P., Rose, S. J., & Hanson, A. R. (2012). Certificates: Gateway to gainful employment and college degrees. Retrieved from: https://cew.georgetown.edu/report/certificates/

Carnevale, A. P., Smith, N., & Strohl, J. (2010). Help wanted: Projections of job and education requirements through 2018. Lumina Foundation.

Center for Law and Social Policy (CLASP) (2016). Funding Career Pathways: A Federal Funding Toolkit For State and Local/Regional Career Pathway Partnerships. Retrieved from: http://www.clasp.org/resources-and-publications/ publication-1/Career-Pathways-Funding-Toolkit-2015-8.pdf

Choitz, V., Soares, L., & Pleasants, R. (2010). A new national approach to career navigation for working learners. Published by the Center for American Progress (CAP). Retrieved from: http://www.jff.org/publications/new-national-approach-career-navigation-working-learners

Christensen, C. M., Baumann, H., Ruggles, R., & Sadtler, T. M. (2006). Disruptive innovation for social change. Harvard business review, 84(12), 94.

Community Research Partners. (2008). Ohio stackable certificates: models for success. Columbus, OH: Author. Retrieved from: http://www. workingpoorfamilies.org/pdfs/Ohio_Stackable.pdf

Corporation for a Skilled Workforce (CSW), (2014). Call for a National Conversation on Creating a Competency-based Credentialing Ecosystem. Ann Arbor, MI: Author. Retrieved from: http://skilledwork.org/wp-content/ uploads/2014/05/2014-04-18-Developing-a-Competency-Based-Credentialing-Ecosystem.pdf

CSW. (2013). Making a Market for Competency Based Credentials. Ann Arbor, MI: Author. Retrieved from: http://skilledwork.org/publications/making-a-market/

Ganzglass, E., Bird, K., & Prince, H. (2011). Giving Credit where Credit Is Due: Creating a Competency-Based Qualifications Framework for Postsecondary Education and Training. Center for Law and Social Policy, Inc.(CLASP). Retrieved from: http://www.clasp.org/resources-and-publications/files/Giving-Credit.pdf

Hanks, A. (2015). Making Pell Work. Washington DC: National Skills Coalition. Retrieved from: http://www.nationalskillscoalition.org/resources/publications/ file/2015-07-Making-Pell-Work-How-Americas-30-Billion-Investment-in-Need-Based-College-Aid-Can-Be-More-Job-Driven.pdf

Holzer, H. J., & Lerman, R. I. (2007). America's forgotten middle-skill jobs. Washington, DC: The Urban Institute.

Human Capital Institute (HCI) (2012). The Business Impact of Talent Intelligence. White River Junction, VT: Author. Retrieved from: http://www.ikgundemi.com/uploads/6/7/8/0/6780997/2012_taleo_intelligence_229.pdf

Jobs for the Future. (2015). Lessons Learned from Accelerating Opportunity. Retrieved from: http://www.jff.org/sites/default/files/publications/materials/Lessons-Learned-From-Accelerating-Opportunity-041315.pdf

Jobs for the Future (2012). The Promise of Career Pathways Systems Change. Boston, MA: Jobs for the Future. Retrieved from: http://www.napaworkforce.org/portals/3/downloads/CareerPathways_JFF_Paper_060112.pdf

Jobs for the Future. (2004) Breaking Through: Helping low-skilled adults enter and succeed in college and careers. Boston, MA: Author. Retrieved from: http://www.jff.org/sites/default/files/BT_description_one_pager_010411.pdf

Kania, J. and Kramer, M. (Winter 2011) "Collective Impact." Stanford Social Innovation Review, 36–41. Retrieved from: http://ssir.org/articles/entry/collective_impact

Kis, V. and Field, S. (2013). Time for the U.S. to Reskill? What The Survey Of Adult Skills Says. Organisation for Economic Co-operation and Development (OECD). Retrieved from: http://skills.oecd.org/Survey_of_Adult_Skills_US.pdf

Kotter, J. (2012). Leading Change. Boston, MA: Harvard Business School Publishing.

Kotter, J. and Cohen, D. (2012). The Heart of Change. Boston, MA: Harvard Business School Publishing.

Kozumplik, R., Nyborg, A., Garcia, D., Cantu, L., & Larsen, C. (2011, September). Career pathways toolkit: Six key elements of success. Washington, D.C.: Social

Policy Research Associates for the US Department of Labor. Updated 2015.

McPhail, S. M., Ed. (2007). Alternative validation strategies: Developing new and leveraging existing validity evidence. San Francisco, CA: John Wiley & Sons.

Mourshed, M., Farrell, D., & Barton, D. (2012). Education to employment: Designing a system that works. Boston, MA: National Partnership for Educational Access. Retrieved from: https://npeac.memberclicks.net/assets/education%20to%20employment_final.pdf

National Commission on Adult Literacy, (2008). Reach Higher, America: Overcoming Crisis in the U.S. Workforce. New York, NY: Council for the Advancement of Adult Literacy. Retrieved from: http://www.nationalcommissiononadultliteracy.org/ReachHigherAmerica/ReachHigher.pdf

National Network (2015). Work-and-learn in action. Retrieved from: http://www.nationalnetwork.org/wp-content/uploads/2015/05/walguidebook.pdf

National Network of Sector Partners (NNSP) (2010). Sector Snapshot: a profile of sector initiatives. Insight: Center for Community Economic Development. Retrieved from: http://www.insightcced.org/press-room/publications/workforce-development-2/

Naughton, J. and Knapp, L. (2010). Certificate or Credential: that is the question. Association for Talent Development. Retrieved from: https://www.td.org/Publications/Magazines/TD/TD-Archive/2010/11/Certificate-or-Certification-That-Is-the-Question

Roberts, R. and Price, D. (2015). Shifting Gears: Evaluation synopsis. Chicago, IL: Joyce Foundation. Retrieved from: http://www.joycefdn.org/assets/1/7/ShiftingGearsEvaluationSynopsis.pdf.

Rutschow, E. Z., & Crary-Ross, S. (2014). Beyond the GED: Promising Models for Moving High School Dropouts to College. MDRC. Retrieved from: http://files.eric.ed.gov/fulltext/ED545454.pdf

Soricone, L. (2015). Systems Change in the National Fund for Workforce Solutions. Boston, MA: National Fund for Workforce Solutions. Retrieved from:

Uniform Guidelines on Employee Selection Procedures (1978). 43.166 Federal Register 38290-38315.

US Chamber of Commerce Foundation. (2015). Building the talent pipeline: An implementation guide. Washington D.C. Retrieved from: https://www.uschamberfoundation.org/reports/building-talent-pipeline-implementation-guide

US Chamber of Commerce Foundation. (2014). Managing the talent pipeline: An implementation guide. Washington D.C. Retrieved at: https://www.uschamberfoundation.org/talent-pipeline-management-white-paper

Vandal, B. (2009). Revving the education engine. Education Commission of the States and KnowledgeWorks Foundation.

Appendix C

Joint Letter on Career Pathways (2016)

In 2016, the following federal agencies released an updated version of a 2012 joint letter promoting "the use of career pathways approaches as a promising strategy to help adults acquire marketable skills and industry-recognized credentials":

- U.S. Department of Agriculture
- U.S. Department of Commerce
- U.S. Department of Defense
- U.S. Department of Education
- U.S. Department of Energy
- U.S. Department of Health and Human Services
- U.S. Department of Housing and Urban Development
- U.S. Department of Justice
- U.S. Department of Labor
- U.S. Department of Transportation
- U.S. Social Security Administration

Because the MRI is in fundamental alignment with the aims and strategies promoted in the letter, we wish to quote the main text of the letter in full:

In April 2012, the U.S. Departments of Labor, Education, and Health and Human Services formed a Federal partnership and issued a letter of joint commitment to promote the use of career pathways to assist youth and adults with acquiring marketable skills and industry-recognized credentials through better alignment of education, training and employment, and human and social services among public agencies and with employers. In 2013, the U.S. Department of Transportation joined the partnership to advance career pathways in response to the anticipated hiring needs in the transportation sector.

Today, our Federal partnership has grown to include the agencies that are part of the Administration's Skills Working Group (Working Group). This group, launched in November 2014 by U.S. Secretary of Labor Tom Perez, maintains momentum for the Administration's Job-Driven Training Initiative, which seeks to assure that youth and adults completing our education and training programs have the skills businesses need. The Working Group comprises the White House National Economic Council, the Office of Management and Budget, and thirteen Federal agencies, including: the U. S. Departments of Agriculture, Commerce, Defense, Education, Energy, Health and Human Services, Housing and Urban Development, Interior, Justice, Labor, the Social Security Administration, Transportation, and Veterans Affairs (the Departments). The Working Group coordinates activities across these various agencies, including efforts to ensure that career pathways are available to all individuals, especially our nation's low-skilled youth and adults, many of whom are already in the workplace.

This letter, which demonstrates the continued commitment of the Administration to promote career pathways, provides updated information and resources from the expanded Federal partnership to help States, regions, local entities, and tribal communities integrate service delivery across Federal and State funding streams. This letter also ensures that interested partners and agencies—whether focused on education, workforce development, or human and social services—are aware of this joint commitment for improved collaboration and coordination across programs and funding sources.

As the demand for skilled workers increases, some skilled jobs remain unfilled. In an effort to meet the demand for a skilled workforce, the Departments of the expanded Federal partnership have consistently articulated the need for increasing the skills of American workers, including adults and youth with disabilities, and invested in education and training as an economic and business imperative. Despite these efforts, and at the current rate of postsecondary graduation, this country will lack over three million postsecondary graduates to fill those jobs by 2018.

Too often, our systems for preparing low-skilled youth and adults with marketable and in-demand skills can be complex and difficult to navigate for students, job seekers, and employers. Career pathways can offer an efficient and customer-centered approach to training and education by connecting the necessary adult basic education, occupational training, postsecondary education, career and academic advising, and supportive services for students to prepare for, obtain, and progress in a career. The newly-enacted Workforce Innovation and Opportunity Act (WIOA) of 2014 includes an updated definition and overarching framework for the implementation of career pathways at Federal, State, local, and tribal levels. WIOA defines a career pathway as "a combination of rigorous and high-quality education, training, and other services that—

(A) aligns with the skill needs of industries in the economy of the State or regional economy involved;

(B) prepares an individual to be successful in any of a full range of secondary or postsecondary education options, including registered apprenticeships;

(C) includes counseling to support an individual in achieving the individual's education and career goals;

(D) includes, as appropriate, education offered concurrently with and in the same context as workforce preparation activities and training for a specific occupation or occupational cluster;

(E) organizes education, training, and other services to meet the particular needs of an individual in a manner that accelerates the educational and career advancement of the individual to the extent practicable;

(F) enables an individual to attain a secondary school diploma or its recognized equivalent, and at least one recognized postsecondary credential; and

(G) helps an individual enter or advance within a specific occupation or occupational cluster." [Section 3(7) of WIOA]

With this updated definition, the six key elements for developing comprehensive career pathways systems that were included in the April 2012 letter still apply and provide a framework for building an integrated career pathway system: (1) build cross-agency partnerships; (2) identify

industry sector and engage employers; (3) design education and training programs; (4) identify funding needs and sources; (5) align policies and programs; and (6) measure system change and performance. The Departments encourage State, local, and tribal policymakers to use these elements to promote alignment among their public workforce, education, and social and human services systems.

_____

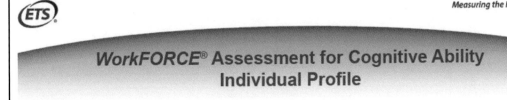

Appendix D

ETS WorkFORCE Assessment for Cognitive Ability

(ETS)   *Measuring the Power of Learning.*®

WorkFORCE® Assessment for Cognitive Ability
Individual Profile

Candidate Name: Jane Doe
Applicant Tracking ID: 1234-5678
Candidate ID: 1234-5678

Date Test Started: 9/15/16
Date Test Completed: 9/15/16
Client: XYZ Corporation

Results Summary:

Reading Prose	Level 1	Level 2	**310** Level 3	Level 4	Level 5
Reading Documents	Level 1	**255** Level 2	Level 3	Level 4	Level 5
Quantitative	Level 1	Level 2	Level 3	**350** Level 4	Level 5

About This Report

The *WorkFORCE*® Assessment for Cognitive Ability gives you information about a candidate's skills in three different areas of ability: Reading Prose, Reading Documents and Quantitative. It also lets you know whether the candidate has the general comprehension, reasoning and quantitative skills necessary to perform successfully in this role.

Scores on the *WorkFORCE*® Assessment for Cognitive Ability range from 0 to 500. This report explains:

- the meaning of Reading Prose, Reading Documents and Quantitative research

- what the candidate's score level means in each area of ability

- what kinds of tasks the candidate can probably do at their level, and areas in which they might work to increase their skills

The candidate's Reading Prose, Reading Documents and Quantitative reports follow.

Individual Profile

WorkFORCE® Assessment for Cognitive Ability

READING PROSE DETAILED REPORT

Candidate Name: Jane Doe
Applicant Tracking ID: 1234-5678
Candidate ID: 1234-5678

Date Test Started: 9/15/16
Date Test Completed: 9/15/16
Client: XYZ Corporation

Reading Prose Score:

310
LEVEL 3

Your Reading Prose score is in the **Level 3** range on Workforce for Cognitive Ability. At this level, you have the skills to cope with most demands of everyday life. You might sometimes find it challenging to use your skills with very unfamiliar, long or complex texts.

What is Reading Prose Skill?

Reading Prose skill involves understanding and using information found in materials such as newspaper articles, brochures, magazine articles, novels, manuals or flyers. All of these materials are examples of prose texts. Texts is a word for printed or written materials of all types.

You are using Reading Prose skills when you:

- Learn ways to quit smoking from a brochure at your health clinic
- Read a story or poem to a child
- Follow instructions in an owner's manual for assembling a product

Skills and Recommendations:

Current Skills

In general, you can usually do things like:

- Understanding and using a variety of reading materials, including newspaper and magazine articles, textbooks, manuals, brochures and flyers.
- Making inferences based on information in reading material by figuring out information that is not clearly and directly stated — in other words, "reading between the lines."
- Interpreting what you read and finding supporting examples.
- Locating information that is found in a few different sentences or paragraphs rather than in a single sentence — for example, finding three fire safety hazards explained in several different paragraphs of a home safety brochure.

Sample task you would be likely to successfully complete:

- Explaining two safety features a bicycle helmet should have using an article in which that information is not labeled as "safety features."

Skills to Strengthen

- Understanding and using long and complicated printed materials.
- Comparing and contrasting information in longer reading materials.
- Being able to summarize information you read.

Skills to Build in the Future

- Using prose texts to answer questions with multiple conditions — for example, finding a job listed in the want ads that meets three conditions: flexible hours, good hourly wage and location close to home.
- Interpreting information and ideas contained in various types of reading materials.
- Using background knowledge of different topics to facilitate and enhance your understanding of what you read.
- Being able to integrate information you read.

CONFIDENTIAL

Individual Profile

WorkFORCE® Assessment for Cognitive Ability

READING DOCUMENTS DETAILED REPORT

Candidate Name: Jane Doe
Applicant Tracking ID: 1234-5678
Candidate ID: 1234-5678

Date Test Started: 9/15/16
Date Test Completed: 9/15/16
Client: XYZ Corporation

Reading Documents Score: **255 LEVEL 2**

Your Reading Documents score is in the **Level 2** range on Workforce for Cognitive Ability. At this level, you often use your Reading Documents skills successfully. In your current situation at work, at home and in your community, you are most likely able to get by most of the time. However, you probably find it difficult to complete tasks using unfamiliar or complicated documents.

What is Reading Documents Skill?

Reading Documents skill involves finding and using information in forms, schedules, graphs maps, charts and tables.

You are using Reading Documents skills when you:
- Fill out a job application or complete a medical form
- Use a bus schedule to figure out when the next bus will arrive
- Find out today's weather using a weather map
- Use a TV schedule to find out when a favorite TV show starts
- Use an inventory sheet to check warehouse stock at work

Skills and Recommendations:

Current Skills

In general, you can usually do things like:
- Finding one or more pieces of information in basic documents.
- Finding needed information even when there is other similar information in a document — for example, looking through a table of cities and ZIP codes to find a ZIP code you need to mail a letter.

Sample task you would be likely to successfully complete:
- Finding the prices of several specific items on a menu.

Skills to Strengthen
- Using several pieces of information provided to complete a form.
- Comparing information in different parts of a document by looking for similarities.
- Finding multiple pieces of information in a variety of documents.

Skills to Build in the Future
- Using a greater variety of basic documents, including more complicated graphs and tables.
- Integrating information in a document.
- Interpreting graphs and tables, making inferences based on information in the documents.
- Finding information in a table even when similar but incorrect information is located in the same row or column as the correct answer.
- Using documents to answer questions with multiple conditions.

 Individual Profile

WorkFORCE® Assessment for Cognitive Ability

QUANTITATIVE DETAILED REPORT

Candidate Name: Jane Doe
Applicant Tracking ID: 1234-5678
Candidate ID: 1234-5678

Date Test Started: 9/15/16
Date Test Completed: 9/15/16
Client: XYZ Corporation

Quantitative Score: **350** LEVEL 4

Your Quantitative score is in the **Level 4** range on Workforce for Cognitive Ability. At this level, you have the skills to cope with most of the quantitative demands of everyday life. When you need to figure out something, you can usually find the numbers you want in document or prose materials. As long as you don't have to go through too many complicated steps, you can typically manage your quantitative needs.

What is Quantitative Skill?

Quantitative skill involves using numbers found in ads, forms, flyers, articles and other printed materials and then adding, subtracting multiplying, dividing or doing other math to get the information you need.

You are using Quantitative skills when you:

- Add up how much you save when you use coupons to buy two items at a store
- Keep score for your bowling team
- Figure out the difference between your gross and net pay on your pay check
- Use the instructions on a can of paint to figure out how many cans you need to paint a room

Skills and Recommendations:

Current Skills

In general, you can usually do things like:

- Performing quantitative tasks using numbers found in basic printed materials as well as graphs and tables.
- Deciding what operation to perform (addition, subtraction, multiplication or division) when it is not clearly stated or shown.
- Completing tasks using three or more numbers.
- Performing two or more sequential operations

Sample task you would be likely to successfully complete:

- Calculating correct change by totaling the cost of a meal from a menu and subtracting the total from the specified amount paid.

Skills to Strengthen

- Using prior knowledge in solving mathematical problems — for example, knowing the steps involved to find the average of several numbers or knowing how to convert a decimal number to a percent.

Skills to Build in the Future

- Performing quantitative tasks using numbers found in very complex printed materials.
- Solving mathematical problems that require a sequence of steps.
- Using background knowledge to determine the quantities or operations needed.

CONFIDENTIAL

Appendix E

ETS WorkFORCE Assessment for Job Fit

ETS   *Measuring the Power of Learning.™*

WorkFORCE® Assessment for Job Fit
Individual Profile

Job:	Dieticians and Nutritionists
Candidate Name :	Jane Doe
Applicant Tracking ID:	

Test Date:	16 February 2016
Client:	ABC General Hospital
Registration ID:	7700000000368357

About This Report

The **WorkFORCE®** Assessment for Job Fit is designed to improve workplace productivity by helping identify candidates who are most likely to succeed in your organization. An Expected Job Fit Indicator is provided and ranges from 0 to 100. Scoring algorithms are built based on the job fit scores and job performance of successfully employed individuals in jobs similar to the one for which you are hiring.

Expected Job Fit Indicator:

The Expected Job Fit indicator is intended to provide a general indication of how well a candidate might perform on this job. It is important to recognize that small differences between indicator values are not very meaningful in terms of actual differences in expected job performance. Please refer to **Interpreting the Expected Job Fit Indicator** in your Score User Guide for some more details.

The Expected Job Fit Indicator is not an average, and is calculated using weighted values.

90
Out of 100

ETS

INDIVIDUAL PROFILE

WorkFORCE® Assessment for Job Fit

Jane Doe
Job: Dieticians and Nutritionists
Applicant Tracking ID:

Test Date: 16 February 2016
Client: ABC General Hospital
Registration ID: 7700000000368357

Behavioral Competencies:

Competency / Attribute	Low descriptor	Score	High descriptor
Initiative & Perseverance	Needs direction, may give up easily	R4	Self-starter, drives to get work accomplished
Diligence	Prefers less work and looks for easiest path/solution	R4	Hardworking, ambitious, confident and resourceful
Assertiveness	Passive, has less need to exert control over others	R3	Direct, decisive, persuasive, authoritative
Dependability	Less concerned with community and less reliable	R5	Reliable, punctual, cooperative and has sense of accountability
Responsibility	Not constrained by rules, lacks responsibility	R5	Responsible, adheres to company policy
Dependability	Less concerned with community and less reliable	R5	Reliable, punctual, cooperative and has sense of accountability
Organization	Disorganized with low attention to detail	R3	Manages tasks/activities in an orderly fashion and maintains neat surroundings
Self-Discipline	Disorganized, spontaneous and more easily distracted	R5	Cautious, levelheaded, patient and delays gratification
Teamwork & Citizenship	May prefer to work alone	R2	Works well with groups, prefers teamwork
Generosity	Hesitates to share and self-focused	L1	Shares time and resources
Collaboration	Skeptical, suspicious and confrontational	R5	Trusting, non-critical, cordial and easy to get along with
Caring & Compassion	Less interested in others' experiences and more self-centered	R4	Values the experiences of and establishes deeper connections with others; treating others sensitively
Collaboration	Skeptical, suspicious and confrontational	R5	Trusting, non-critical, cordial and easy to get along with
Calmness	More prone to ranges of emotions when threatened or challenged	R3	Remains calm and stable, even when threatened or challenged
Compassion	Less interested in others' problems and may not connect well with people	R4	Considerate, affectionate, and natural listener or confidant
Problem Solving & Ingenuity	Lacks self-direction and outside-of-the-box thinking	R2	Uses knowledge and facts to solve problems
Intellectual Orientation	Has difficulty in understanding new things	R3	Intellectual and quick to process new information
Inquisitiveness	Less interested in learning new things	R2	Inquisitive and highly perceptive
Creativity	Tends to rely on the ideas of others and keeping the status quo	L1	Inventive and enjoys making improvements
Flexibility & Resilience	May be deeply affected by stress and negativity	R2	Handles stress and ambiguity well
Optimism	Pessimistic and may have a negative outlook	L1	Happy, joyful and has a positive outlook
Stability	Restless, self-conscious and apprehensive	R3	Self-assured, relaxed and confident

Note: Placement of the box with score indicates the strength of the attribute in either direction. A box with score that falls further to the left (L) or right (R) is not necessarily better or worse, but must be interpreted with respect to the specific job demands. The key, below, shows all the possible scores.

L5 L4 L3 L2 L1 | R1 R2 R3 R4 R5

Page 2 of 3

WorkFORCE® Assessment for Job Fit

Behavioral Competencies

Initiative & Perseverance	Initiative and perseverance (diligence, assertiveness, dependability). Reflecting behaviors formally recognized as part of job duties and that contribute to assigned work; completing tasks efficiently and accurately; acting as a self-starter; driving to get work accomplished.
Responsibility	Responsibility (dependability, organization, self-discipline). Conducting oneself with responsibility, accountability and excellence; adhering to organizational policies; being sensitive to and following safety and other regulatory rules and procedures; demonstrating appropriate workplace behavior and conduct.
Teamwork & Citizenship	Teamwork and citizenship (collaboration, generosity). Working with diverse groups of peers and colleagues; contributing to groups; having a healthy respect for different opinions, customs and preferences; participating in group decision making.
Caring & Compassion	Caring and compassion (compassion, collaboration, calmness). Using a people-centric view to understand and value others' experiences; establishing deeper connections with people by listening to and respecting individual needs; selflessly responding to and treating others with appropriate sensitivity and thoughtfulness.
Problem Solving & Ingenuity	Problem solving and ingenuity (creativity, intellectual orientation, inquisitiveness). Using knowledge, facts and data to effectively solve problems; thinking critically and creatively; using good judgment when making decisions; being a self-directed learner.
Flexibility & Resilience	Flexibility and resilience (stability, optimism). Adjusting well to changing or ambiguous work environments; handling stress; accepting criticism and feedback from others; being positive even when facing setbacks.

Personality Attributes

Diligence	Diligence describes behaviors associated with working toward goals and other positive outcomes. Individuals who are high in diligence tend to be described as hardworking, ambitious, confident and resourceful. Individuals who are low in diligence tend to be content with getting by with a minimal amount of work and look for the easiest path/solution.
Assertiveness	Assertiveness describes behaviors associated with being direct and decisive. Individuals who are high in assertiveness tend to be domineering, take-charge people and are often called natural leaders by their peers. Individuals who are low in assertiveness tend to be more passive and do not have a strong need to exert their own personal influence on other people and events.
Dependability	Dependability describes behaviors related to a sense of duty or being answerable for one's behavior. Individuals who are high in dependability like to be of service to others, frequently contribute their time and money to community projects and tend to be cooperative and dependable. Individuals who are low in dependability tend to be less concerned with the community and not someone considered by friends to be reliable.
Organization	Organization describes behaviors related to the ability to plan and organize tasks and activities. Individuals who are high in organization tend to have a strong ability to organize tasks and activities and the desire to maintain neat and clean surroundings. Individuals who are low in organization tend to be more disorganized, have a cluttered work space and do not keep detailed schedules or plans.
Self-Discipline	Self-discipline describes behaviors centered on impulsiveness, the ability to focus on tasks without distraction and the consideration of consequences before taking action. Individuals who are high in self-discipline tend to be cautious, levelheaded, able to delay gratification and patient. Individuals who are low in self-discipline tend to be impulsive, spontaneous and easily distracted.
Generosity	Generosity describes behaviors associated with activities such as helping and doing things for others, giving to charity and volunteering for community improvement. Individuals who are high in generosity tend to share their time and resources. Individuals who are low in generosity hesitate to share and are self-focused.
Collaboration	Collaboration describes behaviors centered on a desire to work or act with others for a common benefit. Individuals who are high in collaboration tend to be trusting, cordial, noncritical and easy to get along with. Individuals who are low in collaboration tend to be skeptical, suspicious and even confrontational.
Calmness	Calmness describes behaviors associated with mood and strong emotions. Individuals who are high in terms of calmness tend to be calm and stable, even when threatened. Individuals who are low in terms of calmness tend to experience a range of negative emotions such as irritability, anger, or hostility.
Compassion	Compassion describes behaviors that may be social or non-social. Individuals who are high in compassion are "there for you whenever you need them." Such individuals are natural listeners and confidants. Individuals who are low on compassion tend to not be interested in others' problems and may not connect easily with people.
Intellectual Orientation	Intellectual orientation involves interest and comfort with intellectual and conceptual matters. Individuals who are high in intellectual orientation are able to process information quickly and would be described by others as knowledgeable, astute and intellectual. Individuals who are low in intellectual orientation tend to have difficulty understanding new things.
Inquisitiveness	Inquisitiveness describes behaviors directed toward understanding how the world works. Individuals who are high in inquisitiveness would be characterized as curious and perceptive; they may read popular science/mechanics magazines and be interested in experimenting with objects and substances to understand how things work. Individuals who are low in inquisitiveness tend to be less interested in understanding how things work and do not spend a lot of time learning new things.
Creativity	Creativity describes behaviors associated with imagination and original thinking. Individuals who are high in creativity tend to be inventive and enjoy making improvements to things. Individuals who are low in creativity are not very creative and tend to rely on other people's ideas.
Optimism	Optimism describes behaviors associated with an individual's general emotional tone and world outlook. Individuals who are high in optimism tend to be happy and joyful and have a positive outlook. Individuals who are low in optimism are pessimistic and may have a negative outlook.
Stability	Stability describes behaviors associated with various degrees of insecurity and anxiety. Individuals who are high in stability tend to be selfassured, relaxed and confident. Individuals who are low in stability are restless, self-conscious and apprehensive in most contexts.

Appendix F

ETS WorkFORCE Assessment for Career Development

Measuring the Power of Learning.™

WorkFORCE® Assessment for Career Development
Work Readiness Profile

Candidate Name: RemiPPV etms PPV testing
Applicant Tracking ID:
Candidate ID: 44224

Test Date: 08 January 2017
Client: ETS PPV-Tier-Client
Registration ID: 0000000000056053

About This Report

The **WorkFORCE®** Assessment for Career Development is designed to improve workplace productivity by helping to identify employees' level of strength in six behavioral competencies, which are comprised of thirteen individual attributes that relate to likelihood of success in each competency, and in performing different tasks within the workplace.

Scores on the **WorkFORCE®** Assessment for Career Development are measured on a scale of Low, Moderate and High levels of strength. This report describes your employees' strengths in these competencies

Work Readiness Index:

The Work Readiness Indicator is intended to provide an indication of general measure of work readiness that will enable employees to gauge their standing relative to currently employed individuals in occupations with similar vocational, educational training, and experience demands. Higher scores indicate more work readiness.

40

The Work Readiness Indicator ranges from 20-80 with 5-point increments based on a T-score distribution, where 50 is the average Work Readiness Indicator of a working population of US adults ranging across zone 2-4 jobs. The standard deviation is 10, so that meaningful differences begin at 5 points.

WorkFORCE® Assessment for Career Development

REPORT SUMMARY

RemiPPV etms PPV testing
Applicant Tracking ID:
Candidate ID: 44224

Test Date: 08 January 2017
Client: ETS PPV-Tier-Client
Registration ID: 0000000000056053

Behavioral Competencies:

Initiative & Perseverance
Diligence + Assertiveness + Dependability

Responsibility
Dependability + Organization + Self Discipline

Teamwork & Citizenship
Collaboration + Generosity

Customer Service Orientation
Collaboration + Generosity + Friendliness

Problem Solving & Ingenuity
Creativity + Intellectual Orientation + Inquisitiveness

Flexibility & Resilience
Stability + Optimism

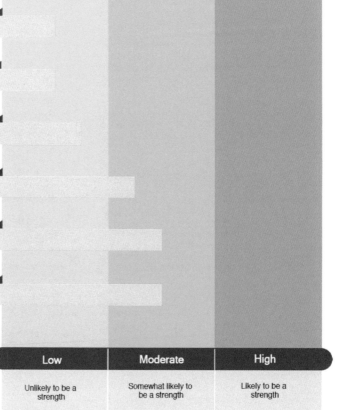

Low	Moderate	High
Unlikely to be a strength	Somewhat likely to be a strength	Likely to be a strength

CONFIDENTIAL

INDIVIDUAL REPORT

INDIVIDUAL REPORT

WorkFORCE® Assessment for Career Development

REPORT DETAILS

RemiPPV etms PPV testing
Applicant Tracking ID:
Candidate ID: 44224

Test Date: 08 January 2017
Client: ETS PPV-Tier-Client
Registration ID: 0000000000056053

Behavioral Competencies:

Initiative & Perseverance

Low — *Unlikely to be a strength*

Reflecting behaviors formally recognized as part of job duties and which contribute to assigned work; completing tasks efficiently and accurately; acting as a self-starter; driving to get work accomplished

The attributes that comprise this behavioral competency are:
Diligence + Assertiveness + Dependability

Click "View Details" to better understand your scores.

View Details >

Attribute	Strength			
	Low	Moderate	High	
Diligence				Low

High scoring individuals are seen as hard working, ambitious, confident, and resourceful.

| **Assertiveness** | | | | Moderate |

High scoring individuals are seen as direct, decisive, and persuasive, and enjoy being in positions of authority and responsibility.

| **Dependability** | | | | Low |

High scoring individuals are reliable, punctual, and cooperative; they have a sense of accountability to others.

Responsibility

Low — *Unlikely to be a strength*

Conducting oneself with accountability and excellence; working in a focused, organized, careful manner; following safety and other regulatory rules, procedures, and policies; demonstrating appropriate workplace behavior and conduct

The attributes that comprise this behavioral competency are:
Dependability + Organization + Self Discipline

Click "View Details" to better understand your scores.

View Details >

Attribute	Strength			
	Low	Moderate	High	
Dependability				Low

High scoring individuals are reliable, punctual, and cooperative; they have a sense of accountability to others.

| **Organization** | | | | Moderate |

High scoring individuals manage tasks and activities in an orderly manner and maintain neat and clean surroundings.

| **Self Discipline** | | | | Low |

High scoring individuals exercise caution, are levelheaded, able to delay gratification, and patient.

Continued on following page...

INDIVIDUAL REPORT

WorkFORCE® Assessment for Career Development

REPORT DETAILS

RemiPPV etms PPV testing
Applicant Tracking ID:
Candidate ID: 44224

Test Date: 08 January 2017
Client: ETS PPV-Tier-Client
Registration ID: 0000000000056053

Behavioral Competencies *(Continued from previous page):*

Teamwork & Citizenship

Low   *Unlikely to be a strength*

Working with diverse groups of peers and colleagues; contributing to groups; having a healthy respect for different opinions, customs and preferences; participating in group decision making

The attributes that comprise this behavioral competency are:
Collaboration + Generosity

Click "View Details" to better understand your scores.

View Details >

Attribute	Strength			
	Low	Moderate	High	
Collaboration				Low

High scoring individuals are pleasant, trusting, and non-critical, and are easy to get along with.

Generosity				Moderate

High scoring individuals are helpful to others; they share time and resources and work with the interest of others in mind.

Customer Service Orientation

Moderate   *Somewhat likely to be a strength*

Conducting oneself in a courteous, patient, and cooperative manner with clients or customers; acting to meet client needs; following through with clients to get the job done well; managing difficult people and assignments; putting the customer first

The attributes that comprise this behavioral competency are:
Collaboration + Generosity + Friendliness

Click "View Details" to better understand your scores.

View Details >

Attribute	Strength			
	Low	Moderate	High	
Collaboration				Low

High scoring individuals are pleasant, trusting, and non-critical, and are easy to get along with.

Generosity				Moderate

High scoring individuals are helpful to others; they share time and resources and work with the interest of others in mind.

Friendliness				Moderate

High scoring individuals are outgoing and gregarious, and enjoy socializing and meeting new people.

Continued on following page...

Page 3 of 4

ETS

INDIVIDUAL REPORT

WorkFORCE® Assessment for Career Development

REPORT DETAILS

RemiPPV etms PPV testing
Applicant Tracking ID:
Candidate ID: 44224

Test Date: 08 January 2017
Client: ETS PPV-Tier-Client
Registration ID: 0000000000056053

Behavioral Competencies *(Continued from previous page):*

Problem Solving & Ingenuity

Moderate *Somewhat likely to be a strength*

Using knowledge, facts, and data to effectively complete challenging tasks; thinking critically and creatively; using good judgment when making decisions; being a self-directed learner

The attributes that comprise this behavioral competency are:
Creativity + Intellectual Orientation + Inquisitiveness

Click "View Details" to better understand your scores.

View Details >

Attribute	Strength			
	Low	Moderate	High	
Creativity				Moderate

High scoring individuals are inventive and capable of thinking "outside of the box."

| Intellectual Orientation | | | | Moderate |

High scoring individuals process new information quickly; they are perceived as knowledgeable and astute.

| Inquisitiveness | | | | Moderate |

High scoring individuals are curious and perceptive, and are interested in learning new information and the way things work.

Flexibility & Resilience

Moderate *Somewhat likely to be a strength*

Adjusting well to changing or ambiguous work environments; handling stress; accepting criticism and feedback from others; being positive, even when facing setbacks

The attributes that comprise this behavioral competency are:
Stability + Optimism

Click "View Details" to better understand your scores.

View Details >

Attribute	Strength			
	Low	Moderate	High	
Stability				High

High scoring individuals work well with changing and evolving work priorities and manage stress well.

| Optimism | | | | Low |

High scoring individuals have a positive outlook, incorporate feedback well, and cope effectively with setbacks.

Work Readiness Index (WRI)

$M = 50, SD = 10$

"Task Proficiency, Effort, and Personal Discipline"

Reflects Areas for Improvement

Typical Work Readiness Profile of Incumbent Employees

Reflects Above Average Strengths

20	25	30	35	40	45	50	55	60	65	70	75	80
○	○	○	○	●	●	●	●	●	*	*	*	*

Behavioral Descriptions

Laidback work style, prone to procrastination, prefers quick/easy solutions, less drive to push one's abilities beyond minimum acceptable standards.	**Diligence**	Prefers to push the boundaries of one's abilities, self-motivated, highly ambitious and goal oriented.
Lack of urgency, prefers positions with less responsibilities to others, difficulty adhering to a time schedule.	**Dependability**	Committed to following through on responsibilities and commitments, highly reliable, punctual, accountable for one's actions and mistakes.
Prefers "organized chaos" to order/structure, difficulty planning or keeping track of items/events.	**Organized**	Prefers order to chaos, meticulous and logical system of planning/organization, high attention to detail.
Restless, self-conscious, anxious, prone to worry about past or future events.	**Calm Under Stress**	Self-assured, confident, able to compartmentalize negative emotions efficiently.
Prefers independent work environments, critically evaluates others' ideas, competitive, forceful, cautious of others.	**Collaborative**	Strongly prefers working in teams or cooperative work environments, works exceptionally well with others, prefers collaborative decision making.

(ETS) WorkFORCE.

Measuring the Power of Learning.™

Certificate of Achievement

Awarded to

for successfully completing the
WorkFORCE® Readiness Training Program

WorkFORCE.
ASSESSMENT FOR
DEVELOPMENT